WHY SHOULD THE DEVIL HAVE ALL THE GOOD MUSIC?

JESUS MUSIC— WHERE IT BEGAN, WHERE IT IS, AND WHERE IT IS GOING.

PAUL BAKER

Prelude by Pat Boone
Foreword by Larry Norman

D1473999

WORD BOOKS
PUBLISHER
WACO, TEXAS

Errata:

The material which begins on page 199 and ends on page
201, beginning with "In his book . . ." is an erroneous duplica-
tion of the text which begins on page 195 and concludes at the
bottom of page 197.

Why Should the Devil Have All the Good Music?
Copyright © 1979 by Paul Baker.

ISBN 0-8499-2858-3
Library of Congress Catalog Card Number 78-65815

Printed in the United States of America

Portions of the history of Jesus music as included in this book have
appeared in slightly modified versions in the following publications: *Rock
in Jesus, Right On!, Harmony,* and *Contemporary Christian Music.*
   All secular record chart numbers included in this history are as tabulated
in *Joel Whitburn's Top Pop Records 1955—1978 book, compiled from
Billboard's Pop charts. This book is published independently. Write to:
Record Research, P.O. Box 200, Menomonee Falls, WI 53051.*

Contents

Prelude by Pat Boone
Foreword by Larry Norman
Introduction

PART I

1/ "Eve of Destruction"		23
2/ "He's Everything to Me"		33
3/ "Jesus Is Just Alright"		43
4/ "Jesus Christ, S. R. O. (Standing Room Only)"		53
5/ "Little Country Church"		61
6/ "Turn Your Radio On"		75
7/ "Day by Day"		85
8/ "Pass It On"		107
9/ "Fat City"		117
10/ "It's Only Right"		125
11/ "The Rock That Doesn't Roll"		137
12/ "All Day Dinner"		147
13/ "Let Us Be One"		157
14/ "Super Star"		167

PART II

15/ "We Need a Whole Lot More of Jesus and a
    Lot Less Rock and Roll"   181
Epilogue   193

PART III

Appendix A. Religious Songs Which Reached the *Billboard* Top
             100 Pop Charts 1955–1978   205
Appendix B. Hit Songs by Artists Who Also Recorded Jesus
             Music Albums   209
Appendix C. A Complete Listing of All Known Jesus Music
             Recording Artists and the Labels on Which They
             Have Recorded   215
Appendix D. Charts: Gospel Music 1964 and Gospel Music 1979   229
Appendix E. Bibliography and Suggested Reading   231
Notes   233

Prelude

Here's everything you ever wanted to know about Jesus music, and didn't know to ask! Paul has done an amazing and thorough job of researching this whole latter day phenomenon, getting right back to its early well springs in traditional Christian music and tracing each tributary as it flows into the cascading river of living water that Jesus music is becoming.

I find the chronicle very exciting, having been involved in it from one of its earliest stages. I've watched this new crest developing, and have earnestly paddled to try and stay in the sweep of it. I remember being stopped in my tracks the first time I heard Paul Stookey's song, "HYMN." It was sung by a virtually unknown trio of boys at a Youth for Christ beach rally in Florida in the late '60s.

I got goose bumps.

It hit me like a brick, or one of those beach hot dogs. "Of *course*—it's possible! Why not talk to young people about Jesus in their own language, and with the sound of their own music? Why not be completely honest about a human being's search for something real in a world that so often accepts substitutes and dehydrated religion?"

Soon after, I began to hear other songs, and know other Christian artists who were doing just that. Larry Norman and Randy Matthews and Paul Johnson and Jimmy Owens, and on and on. I recorded my own first Jesus music album, and even established a new label, Lamb and Lion Records, to serve as a fresh channel for this modern music.

Like so many, continuing right up until now, I was so frustrated that this wonderful new music couldn't find distribution or air space on the radio. Here was a totally new avenue of Christian expression, one that would communicate immediately with millions of young people in a way they could understand—and nobody knew what to do with it! It was too "religious" for pop stations, and too "pop" for religious stations.

Obviously, new channels would have to open up, and I decided to be one of them. It seems to have been a long and frustrating struggle, but now the doors are opening. More and more Christian stations have accepted Jesus music in its varied forms and are spotlighting the whole galaxy of dedicated and talented new artists. Now, even the secular and rock stations are beginning to perk up their ears and listen to the sound of young people singing about Jesus in a musical form that is every bit as commercial and entertaining and arresting as any of the secular artists.

The tide is irresistible now, and chinks in the dam are appearing everywhere.

In the 96th Psalm, and a number of other places, David cries,

> Sing to the Lord *a new song*:
> sing to the Lord, all the earth.
> Sing to the Lord, praise His name
> Proclaim His salvation day after day.
> Declare His glory among the nations,
> His marvelous deeds *among all peoples*.

On the day of Pentecost, the Bible tells us that "every man heard in his own language."

People used to ask me, "What is this Jesus movement, anyway?" I replied, "It's Jesus moving, that's what it is." No human people originated or organized the Jesus movement; Jesus did it, through yielded young hearts.

Now they're asking, "What is Jesus music anyway?" I reply, "It's Jesus singing, in the hearts of young people by His Spirit!" Again, no person conceived or organized Jesus music, it's just happening in the hearts and talents of young people, and building to an undeniable crescendo of testimony and praise.

I'm grateful to Paul Baker for bringing the whole dynamic history of Jesus music into sharp focus and giving credit where credit is certainly due. Praise the Lord!

Pat Boone,
Beverly Hills, California

Foreword

There was a time I felt quite alone with my music. I had gone forward in church to accept Christ when I was five. I strained to reach the high notes when we sang the hymns and I struggled to understand the lyrics which were filled with things like "bulwarks never failing." If the hymns seemed archaic to me, well that made sense. God was very ancient, too. These hymns were probably written back when he first made the world.

When I was young I heard Elvis Presley sing "Hound Dog" on the radio and I began to wonder why there couldn't be church music that sounded a little more modern. And so I began to write songs in the fourth grade. A few years later I sang "Moses" and some other early songs at the church picnic but I felt embarrassed and just a little angry when no one really understood what I was trying to do.

My father, bless his heart, did not allow me to listen to the radio anymore and tried to "encourage" me to give up music entirely. I was obedient on the first count but couldn't bear to stop writing songs. And so for many years I felt alone in my enthusiasm for Jesus Rock music.

Periodically, I performed in public and upon leaving school I signed with Capitol Records but it was a long time before I met anyone who "understood" me.

Then in 1967 my sister told me about this boy who had seen me perform in concert with my band PEOPLE! and wanted to meet me. I didn't think much about it until one day I came home to find my sister sitting on the couch and heard someone singing in the other room. I walked into the next room and saw this skinny little high school kid singing "Bluebird" at the top of his lungs. I joined in on the harmony.

That's how I met Randy Stonehill. Although it was a few years before he would become a Christian, he identified with Jesus Rock from the time he first heard it. And so, quite suddenly, there seemed to be two of us.

In 1969, after the release of my third album for Capitol (UPON THIS ROCK), it seemed that people were ready for a modern approach to Christian music. Within two years there were a dozen or so groups or solo performers just in California who were recognizably ''contemporary.''

So you can imagine my joy when not too much later I found out there were many more scattered all over America. A disc jockey named Paul Baker had a Jesus Rock radio show and a writer named Brooke Chamberlain had written a few articles about contemporary Christian music—and I met a guy named Frank Edmondson who seemed to know all about Jesus music. He not only ''understood'' it but was explaining it to everyone who came near. Now further imagine my surprise when I found out that not only were Paul Baker and Brooke Chamberlain the same person, but that both of them were also Frank Edmondson.

Frank explained that he had been in radio for a long time and had experimented with different jock ''handles,'' as most disc jockeys do, and that gradually it became convenient to let Paul continue to do the radio show and let Brooke move into writing while he, Frank, remained himself.

When I got to know him better I found out that not only did he have three different names, but he seemed to have the energy of three different people.

He not only had a three hour radio show, every night at one point, but he had started a magazine called *Rock in Jesus*. He wrote it, edited it, printed it, assembled it, stapled it, addressed it, stamped it, and mailed it. He also paid for it. After all, what publisher could be convinced that Jesus Rock was a viable and spiritual art form? Most people seemed convinced that rock and roll was of the devil and that God would never use it.

So Frank stood alone and did it all by himself. He was a tall skinny kid who had great enthusiasm for his belief in Christ and gentle empathy for those who did not believe.

To those who disagreed with his understanding of Christian music he could discuss church history and church music and back the conversation up with that nice smile of his. Not only did he have a nice attitude but he had nice looks too, which helped. . . . I mean it wouldn't be easy to convince a grownup that Jesus Rock was a legitimate direction in Christian music if you looked like a leftist—drugged—burned out—communist—faggott—weirdo.

But for all his rapport with the grownups and the establishment, to me Frank didn't look exactly "straight." He had longish hair and looked like the street people. But because his looks and personality also passed inspection with adults, Frank sat on the borderline and communicated to both sides and helped bring them a little closer together.

By the time Explo '72 occurred in Dallas, Texas, Frank had a wealth of "research" material crammed into his tiny apartment. His clothes remained in drawers or hung over chairs because his closet was filled with records. He had albums and singles stacked every place. He thumbed through them and showed me songs I never heard on any radio show except his. He had songs written by Christians (and others by non-Christians which had only a passing reference to Christ or God), but he had them all! And he knew which was which. He sensed that a very large "Jesus music" culture was going to develop and he was more than prepared for it. It looked to me as though he were the sole historian of a new era in church music.

Frank not only chronicled the Jesus music history in his magazine but he helped to make it. As early as 1971 he was already stretching the dimensions of religious broadcasting by experimenting with its possibilities in format. Besides playing obscure gems from his private record collection, he once set up a room for an audience right in the radio station and had me do a live concert on the air. It was the first time many of my songs had been on the air because I had not previously released them on record. I did "The Tune" that night on his show and though it had never been heard before (or since) on any radio program anywhere, until its release on SOMETHING NEW UNDER THE SON, it suddenly became the most requested song in my concerts. I was amazed at how far-reaching Frank's radio show was in its influence on the grapevine.

There were a few other Christian disc jockeys like Scott Ross who played contemporary Christian music, but none of them were as avant-garde as Frank. None had access to his mammoth collection of records so none had such a staggering playlist of different selections. And none were quite daring enough to risk alienating a religious sponsor or associate with an experimental format, so Frank made important cultural inroads into what Christian radio could become.

I guess I've known Frank for almost nine years now. He kept his radio show going for all those years and later worked for Word Records pioneering radio coordination and format and helping disc jockeys understand how to improve their technique in a field that Frank more or less pioneered—Jesus Rock Radio. And later he was asked to head up the FCCM, the Fellowship of Contemporary Christian Ministries.

Right from the first time I met Frank and heard Paul Baker on the radio and read Brooke's articles in *Rock in Jesus*, I thought Frank should write a book. He finally has.

—LARRY NORMAN

March, 1979

Introduction

I was one of the rock generation. I can still remember "borrowing" my father's turquoise transistor radio (the first such radio I had seen) when he brought it home one day. I don't know if he ever had a *chance* to use it again after that day, either, because everywhere I went thereafter I had it with me, next to my ear.

The music on that radio was usually rock and roll: "Peggy Sue" by Buddy Holly; "Bird Dog" by the Everly Brothers. Why I was attracted to the rock station I can't really say. I had my choice of country, religious, mood music, and rhythm and blues. But, as an adolescent, even though I didn't like *all* of the rock and roll, I guess I was drawn to the energy and excitement which rock music carried inherently.

Bill Haley rocked with his Comets, Elvis Presley rolled out a song about his "Teddy Bear," Jerry Lee Lewis sang about "A Whole Lotta Shakin' Goin' On." Rock music (even the mellowest of rock ballads) became the headache of older Americans. Rock was crude to the older folks, but definitely "cool" to the young people.

The furor over rock and roll music started in the '50s and never really abated until in the late '60s and the early '70s, when adults simply got tired of fighting it. By then, the "beautiful music" of the adults ironically was very often music written and originally performed by rock musicians such as Elvis and the Beatles. When drums and rock rhythm were added to orchestra recordings, the adults somehow didn't seem to mind it as much as they had originally.

I also grew up "in the church." My parents took the whole family to church each week, and I know my personal faith is now as strong as it is because of the Bible study, the worship, and the fellowship I enjoyed there.

Unlike many peers, to whom such music was at the least "foreign," I enjoyed the music of the church. By the time I had reached my high school years, though, I began to yearn for *contemporary* music which conveyed my faith in Jesus. I wanted music I could share with my unchurched friends—music which wasn't strange to them.

I first experienced such music in the form of Christian folk songs, sung on Thursday nights at a "Christian hootenanny" across town from where I lived. While the guitar players and washtub bass "experts" accompanied, we sang songs which I'd sung many times at church fellowships and socials—"Do Lord," "When the Saints Go Marchin' In," "Give Me Oil in My Lamp"—but for some reason they took on a vitality I had never experienced in them before. Somehow, with the guitars and basses, I didn't feel as embarrassed asking my out-of-church schoolmates to join us on Thursdays.

My next encounter with contemporary Christian music came a few years later when I attended the World Baptist Youth Congress in Berne, Switzerland. A smartly uniformed youth choir performed a new musical entitled "Good News" before the 6000 delegates. "Good News" utilized folk music mostly, but even went so far as to put in a few semirock licks which would then and for months to follow drop the jaw of many a staid church member.

Next, it was through a subscription offer in *Campus Life* magazine and membership in Word, Incorporated's "Young America Record Club" that I began amassing a collection of every contemporary and quasi-contemporary Christian music album there was. The names of the performers seem quite tame now: Cliff Barrows and the Gang, The Melody Four Quartet, The Teen Tones. But at the time they were a big step in the direction of new music for Christian young people like myself.

In 1970, a singer named John Fischer came through my hometown of Tampa, Florida, while touring with Evangelist Leighton Ford. I was excited about the music he had performed, so I introduced myself to him and we spent an afternoon together discussing what he kept calling "Jesus music." I liked the expression, and I immediately caught on to using it, just as hundreds of other young people around the country were already doing.

I kept hearing the words "Jesus music" more and more frequently. When a group known as the Pilgrim 20 from Wichita, Kansas, sang it in a Tampa church recreation hall, they called it "Jesus rock." When a group known as the Spurrlows came through town for a performance, it was "sacred music" with a new flair. But it was all *Jesus music* to me.

Those are recollections of my first impressions of a music style which would greatly influence my life. While I was delving deeper and deeper to find more of this exciting, fresh music, thousands of young people across the country were writing it, discovering it, singing it and sharing it.

During the ten years or so covered in this book, I had the good fortune to live in Florida, Kansas, California, Texas, Colorado, and Europe. Living in these geographically extant areas provided grand opportunities for me to observe what was happening in Jesus music, and to be an active part of it all. Thus, this history of Jesus music and the Jesus Movement is a history as I saw it and often participated in it. That is why I occasionally lapse into the first person in the pages that follow.

In 1968, when I first began collecting my Jesus music records and dreaming of what contemporary Christian music could be and could accomplish, I had no idea it would grow as fast as it has. The growth has been literally stupendous. Now that it *has* grown, it's time we learned from the zealousness of the young people in the early days. Even more important, we need to see where, in certain instances, our priorities have been turned topsy-turvy. I hope we can learn from looking back, taking stock, and then moving forward with a renewed vigor and perspective.

Rock music about Jesus hasn't really found favor with adults any more easily than did secular rock. But, regardless of one's stance in the question of Jesus rock music—pro or con—the fact remains that rock music has had the ears of the nation's youth since its inception. Likewise, Jesus music has emanated from people for whom rock music has been a natural language. It has communicated, often where no other language has.

By the time of the writing of this book, there were so many people involved in contemporary Christian music, there was virtually no possible way to chronicle or credit everyone who had a part. Quite honestly, that was the most frustrating part of writing the book. There is a natural tendency for us to venerate the well-known performer and pass over or simply forget the lesser-known musicians who have done the Lord's work just as diligently, but in less visible ways or perhaps on a local basis. In fact, in some cases they were the hardest workers.

For every well-known musician, there is a lesser-known roadie who assists in setting up concerts. Likewise, there is also a person to invite that musician to perform the concert, radio broadcasters to publicize and advertise the concert, people to get the musician to and from the airport, record company personnel to release and record his albums if he records, personnel to promote and publish his music, and so forth, not to mention supportive brothers and sisters praying for him and the audiences who listen to him, and buy his albums if any are available.

Thus, at times, I have spent more time describing the work of people "in the wings" than the people "in the spotlight," for this is mainly a history of the *work* done by people glorifying God through Jesus music, not necessarily the people doing it. Most of the musicians would agree that their names are not so important as the lives changed by their music.

I wish to thank a few of the "anonymous" and better-known people who have helped me through the years in various ways: Dallas Albritton, and Mosie Lister for introducing us; Victor Salem; Henry Webb; Daylon Rushing; Herb Hunt; Dan Vap and the others who helped me with *Rock In Jesus* magazine; Billy Ray Hearn; Larry Norman; Gary Elrod; Mark Puckett; John Grable; John Styll; Erwin Hearne; Bob Freeman; Gary Dick; Freddy Piro; Bob Cotterell; Jack Bailey; Robbie Marshall; and of course, my parents, Frank and Doris Edmondson. Their encouragement, help, and exhortation were invaluable and still are greatly appreciated. Also, I deeply appreciate the many people who have so generously supported my radio show "A Joyful Noise" since it began in 1970.

I owe unending thanks to the scores of people who, in private interviews or casual conversations, helped me so much to recall the important people, places, dates, and events which make up the history of Jesus music.

My appreciation also goes out to Lou and Peggy Hancherick of *Harmony* magazine for their inclusion in the magazine of my articles on the history of Jesus music. Many thanks to Dan Hickling, publisher of the *Foreversong Journal,* for his extensive work on the listing of contemporary albums and artists in Appendix C.

Also, a big thank you to the many people at Word, Incorporated, from the warehouse to the front offices, who made my three and one-half years there so memorable and enjoyable. The biggest thank you of all goes to my wife Debbie, who "inherited" the book, which was in the process of being written when we were wed. Her suggestions were invaluable, her patience was unbelievable, her tolerance was insurpassable, and her assistance, especially those final nights of getting the book finished by working all hours of the night, were the ultimate in selfless giving.

PAUL BAKER

Denver, Colorado
December 30, 1978

Part I

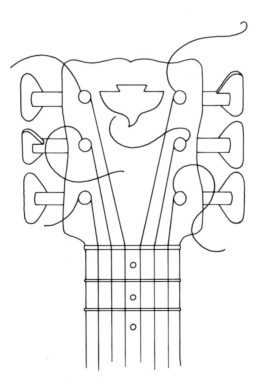

1/

"Eve of Destruction"

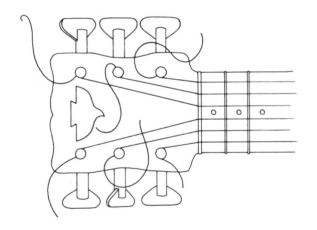

Eastern world, it is exploding
Violence flaring, bullets loading
You're old enough to kill
But not for voting
You don't believe in war
But what's that gun you're toting
And you tell me
You don't believe
We're on the eve of destruction

"Eve of Destruction" by P. F. Sloan
© 1965 American Broadcasting Music, Inc.
Used by permission only. All rights reserved.

The babies born just after World War II came booming into the Sixties and nearly caused a national nervous breakdown. . . . That decade ranks as one of the most convulsive periods of social ferment and change in American history.[1]

HOW WE EVER MADE IT THROUGH THAT DECADE IS A MYSTERY. THE SIXTIES were filled with major sociological problems, and one of the most perplexing was the Generation Gap. America's youth were exasperated with the materialistic living of their elders, the very life-style for which the parents had toiled and struggled so much to give to their children.

In his book, *The Jesus Generation,* Billy Graham said, "We came through the Depression and World War II. Hardship and death made us determined that our children would never have to go through another depression or another war. In pursuit of that goal, we chose the wrong means. Instead of turning to spiritual values, we turned to materialism." [2] Graham added that two of the things which drove so many of the youth into radical fervor and revolutionary fever were "the soulless materialism and the deification of technology in America." [3]

So, the youth reacted by throwing everything back into their parents' faces. They protested wars, greediness, hypocrisy, pollution, bigotry, technology, and the Establishment in general. The noisy radicals, the "stoned" hippies, and the quiet flower children became the revolution.

For the radicals, the solution was to destroy. "Burn baby, burn" was the call to arms. For the less aggressive hippies, the best way to handle everything that was going down was to "get stoned" and escape into the world of drugs. For the flower children, the desired world was one of peace, brotherhood, love and understanding—a sort of "back to the basics" attitude. Their ideals were admirable, but the youth lacked the knowledge of how to realistically live them out.

Many of the youth of each type found themselves searching the teachings of scores of foreign and domestic, ancient and brand-new philosophies, religions and sects. The youth were trying desperately to find answers which technology could not provide, and solutions which American Christianity had failed to convey to them.

In his study of the Generation Gap, Evangelist Billy Graham listed what he felt were the causes of the rift:

> The natural rebellion of the human heart; the emptiness evident everywhere; the constant erosion and dehumiliation of personality by a machine-oriented age; the lack of purpose and meaning; the tragic failure of our educational system which seems more and more to alienate the young and consequently anger their parents; the overriding social problems that have no foreseeable solutions; the failure of government to understand that the basic gut-level problems facing the nation are not materialistic and social but moral and spiritual.[4]

When it came to spiritual values, the young people were more disillusioned than ever. The motto "In God We Trust" seemed to them not a creed but a mockery. The youth were convinced that there must be a better way to do things.

In their zeal to find meaning for their existence, however, the youth hastily concluded that it was "thumbs down" to all of Christianity. They failed to carry their investigations past the obvious mistakes and blunders of some of their Christian parents and the "American" style of Christianity. They failed to realize the source of the faith: Jesus Christ.

Some church leaders saw the increasing friction and tried to alert the established church to the growing chasm between the youth and the establishment. Almost prophetically, author Dennis Benson warned in 1969: "How long will it be before the silent Sunday morning army of youth realize what poor fare it has been fed and will turn away from the church?"[5]

Benson wasn't through. He warned further:

> Youth's orientation asks of the church "How does it smell, feel, sound, or appear?" No longer acceptable are answers such as, "It must taste like communion wafers and grape juice; or it must smell like damp carpeting and moldy basements; or it must feel to the touch like glass beads; or it must sound like songs pitched too high for men to sing and phrased in language too quaint for this age; or it must appear only at a given time during the week in the dress of the ladies and gentlemen."[6]

Not only were the youth growing tired of the hypocrisy in what they saw as Christianity, they were also discouraged by the lack of interest the established church was taking in spiritual matters. In 1971, Norman Vincent Peale admitted:

For years we watched a spiritual vacuum growing in our young people. All the signs were there: dissatisfaction with a materialistic and affluent society; impatience with old forms of worship; a groping for fulfillment—first in rock music, then in various kinds of mysticism, finally in drugs. The churches turned off emotionalism and put all their chips on intellectualizing Christianity. Result: They priced themselves out of the youth market. We saw all this happening. But did we reach out eagerly and offer the seekers a solution they could accept in terms they could understand? I'm afraid many didn't.[7]

There were, fortunately, some youth who did not pass up the possibility that perhaps the trouble with America and American Christianity existed not in the faith's early foundations, but rather in the more recent waverings from the "Gospel Truth." These youth had the maturity to "hang in" with the Christian faith. Rather than break with the church entirely, they began their own movement outside of the church to relate teachings and life styles which they felt more closely paralleled the early church. They sought to "get back to the Bible."

Thus, an "underground church" began again, as it had in the catacombs and private dwellings of centuries before. It had no organization; it consisted of individuals, sometimes thousands of miles apart, who had the same goals: communicating Christ to millions of stranded and confused young people caught in the middle of a Generation Gap, and instilling joy and excitement about true Christian living to the millions of churched young people who had grown tired of church life.

In his book *The Underground Church,* Edward Plowman, a noted historian on the Jesus Movement, observed:

They are not flag-waving destructionists bent on overthrow; basically they seek spiritual renewal and satisfaction for themselves. They hope the wider Church will join their quest. I have found little bitterness among them and almost no inclination to mount a holy war of liberation against the formal church.[8]

The beginning of the Jesus Movement in modern America has been traced back to 1967, when the Christian World Liberation Front opened the first Christian coffeehouse in the Haight-Ashbury district of San Francisco. Haight-Ashbury was a gathering ground for every imaginable type of dissident youth. A freckled street minister, "Holy Hubert" Lindsey preached on the street corners of

Berkeley, telling the dissidents and derelicts alike about Jesus Christ.

As Lindsey recounts it, "In 1965, there were 15,000 rioting students at Berkeley. In 1966, they didn't have a riot at Berkeley. In 1967 we had a revival! We turned that revolution into revival!"

By early 1968 another street preacher, Arthur Blessitt, was spending his Tuesday nights preaching to club-goers at "Gazzarri's Hollywood-A-Go-Go" on Sunset Strip. "I kept going into Gazzarri's trying to witness to him and all the nightclub people," explained Blessitt. "Finally one night, he agreed to let me do a gospel rally. After that, it became a regular weekly thing, 10 to 12 each Tuesday."

Calvary Chapel, a small Orange County church, was beginning to experience growing pains. The congregation was growing so rapidly, a large circus tent had to be raised to house the growing throngs of California youth and adults. Pastor Chuck Smith led his congregation with a special sensitivity for the young people.

Before 1969 had passed, the increased activity of the Christian youth underground also included the publication of newspapers (called "Jesus papers") and their free distribution on street corners and on college and high school campuses. At Berkeley, *Right On!*, the pioneer Jesus paper, debuted as a Christian response to the radical underground *Berkeley Barb*. Twenty thousand copies were distributed. In Seattle, *Agape* hit the streets. *The Hollywood Free Paper*, later to have the largest circulation of any of the papers, was started by former entertainer Duane Pederson in October of 1969. In Spokane, *Truth* began publication.

These papers made no secret that they were Jesus papers. They mainly consisted of testimonies, Bible studies, and comics relating gospel-oriented tales. *Right On!* published from a more intellectual perspective, was devoted to attacking propaganda from radical non-Christian groups.

All of the action wasn't in California, though. In the small berg of Freeville, New York, an ex-rock disc jockey from New York City, Scott Ross, was celebrating his discovery of Christ by broadcasting a radio show on five New York stations from Buffalo to Albany. Ross also founded "Love Inn," an old barn which had been converted in more ways than one. The renovated barn became one of the earlier Christian communities of the Jesus Movement.

In West Palm Beach, Florida, the Movement was gathering

momentum under the auspices of the First Baptist Church. First Baptist had seen the early warning signs of restless youth. Fenton Moorhead, a professor at Palm Beach Atlantic College and specially appointed "Minister to the Generation Gap," was stirring up the enthusiasm of Florida teens. Despite opposition from some church members and West Palm Beach citizens, the youth of the church as well as college students from all over the country were challenged to reach the estimated 40,000 hippies, radicals, flower children, and others who were to attend the 1969 West Palm Beach Rock Festival. The extravaganza featured Janis Joplin, the Jefferson Airplane, the Rolling Stones, and many other top rock performers. Arthur Blessitt led a special training session and then the Christians descended on the festival. The result was an admirable witnessing effort. An estimated 3,000 youth responded by becoming followers of Jesus Christ.

There were plenty of other places where the Spirit was stirring, leading into a climactic decade of spiritual renewal: Dallas, Wichita, Palo Alto, even Waikiki.

Like the waves of Waikiki, the expanse of the Jesus Movement swelled. Sometimes through the efforts of earlier pioneers and sometimes through their own searching, the youth of the Generation Gap began studying the character of Jesus more closely than they had in decades. They found that Jesus Christ had taught the very things for which the youth of the twentieth century were striving.

For these youth, the words of Christ spoken 2,000 years ago could have been spoken just as well in the 1970s. Two thousand years ago, Jesus said of love: "This is my commandment, that ye love one another, as I have loved you." [9] Of peace, Christ preached on the Mount of Olives: "Blessed are the peacemakers: for they shall be called the children of God." [10] On brotherhood, Jesus' advice was: "Whosoever is angry with his brother without a cause shall be in danger of the judgment." [11]

More and more youth were rediscovering the classic words of Jesus of Nazareth. Norman Vincent Peale described it this way:

So what happened? A miracle, in a way. Without much leadership from anywhere, some of these young seekers groped and blundered and fought their way to an encounter with a Person so majestic, so appealing, so loving, so lifegiving that the aching void in their lives was filled with a tremendous explosion of joy. [12]

Joy—the most noticeable attribute of the Jesus people. Even *Time* magazine was impressed: "What startles the outsider is the extraordinary sense of joy that they are able to communicate." [13] Those outsiders, on the whole, welcomed the exuberance of the Jesus people.

By 1971, the "Movement" was going full steam and had drawn the attention of *Time, Life, Look,* CBS-TV, and NBC-TV. Even *Rolling Stone,* the bible of the antiestablishment youth underworld, reported:

> This new-style fundamentalist revival has spread rapidly across the country. "Every day with Jesus is sweeter than the day before," say these mostly young, long-haired children of America: Middleclass teenagers from the suburbs, ex-drug addicts and acid cultists, blacks from big-city ghettos, and babyfaced veterans of Vietnam. All of them born-again Christians. [14]

That was reported in June of 1971, several years before a man named Jimmy Carter would cause world-wide awareness of the term "born again."

Time magazine appeared to have a running commentary of God in American life on its covers. The April 8, 1966 issue of *Time* had sported a cover asking, "Is God Dead?" On the cover of the last issue of 1969, the question had been "Is God Coming Back to Life?" Then, in the same week as the 1971 *Rolling Stone* article on the Jesus Movement, *Time* featured a modernistic cover painting of Jesus and ran a feature article on the "Jesus Revolution." Said *Time*:

> Jesus is alive and well in the radical spiritual fervor of a growing number of young Americans who have proclaimed an extraordinary religious revolution in his name. Their message: the Bible is true, miracles happen, God really did so love the world that he gave it his only begotten son. [15]

Time had answered its own questioning covers.

Miracles come with just about any large spiritual revival, and one of the miracles of the Jesus Revolution was the penetration of its message into so many different types of life styles. The Movement permeated all portions of the youth culture: Satanists, dropouts, rock musicians, flower children, cultists, athletes, students, and even the not-so-rebellious but often apathetic "straight" youth.

Jesus' teachings were as full of salvation for one type of person as for another.

There was the common language of the '60s and '70s youth which assured rapid transmission of "new" ideas. It wasn't so much in the cute cliches of that era: "feelin' groovy," "right on," "far out," and "heavy," though these exclamations were very much a part of the Jesus Movement. It was in the methods of communication. Among the youth, word of Christ was not spread to any great degree over the air-waves or in books, as was so common with many other idealogies or current "fads." The method was ancient—from one person to another. It was an amazing example of the power of "word of mouth" and street witnessing. The message was taken to the streets.

As often as it was spoken, the message was sung. Just as the work of the Spirit knew no boundaries, neither did music. There may have been differences as to what style of music was preferred, but hardly a person did not relate in some way to music. And the people of the Jesus Movement used music to its fullest advantage.

2/
"He's Everything to Me"

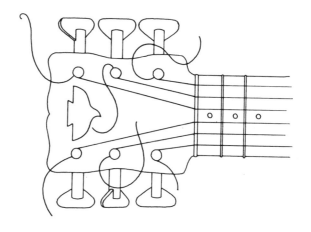

HE'S EVERYTHING TO ME by Ralph Carmichael
In the stars His handiwork I see,
On the wind He speaks with majesty.
Though He ruleth over land and sea,
What is that to me?
I will celebrate Nativity,
For it has a place in history,
Sure, He came to set His people free,
What is that to me?
Till by faith I met Him face to face,
And I felt the wonder of His grace,
Then I knew that He was more than just a God who didn't care, that lived
away out there and,
Now He walks beside me day by day,
Ever watching o'er me lest I stray,
Helping me to find that narrow way,
He's everything to me.

DURING THE EARLY '60S, FOLK SONGS WERE ONE OF THE MOST POPULAR forms of music. While Chubby Checker was twisting and Bobby Rydell was singing "Wild One," folk music "hootenannies" were becoming the Friday night fare on college campuses. Some songsters traveled to the remotest parts of the Appalachians in search of more folk songs that could be recorded, introduced to the public, and in many cases, exploited. But while the raw folk music was touching a limited audience with songs of unrequited love and bluetail flies, needles and pins were being woven into the fabric of the more public folk songs of Joan Baez, Bob Dylan, Ian and Sylvia, and Peter, Paul & Mary. Theirs were the folk songs of protest lamenting the woes of the younger generation as the Gap began widening.

Though folk music was just about the simplest and most innocent form of music in America, the protest songs caused nearly all folk music to fall out of favor with the adults. In their eyes, all of it was lumped into one unacceptable category. Folk music was for beatniks and hippies, not respectable people.

The churches of America continued with the hymns and their own style of folk music, though it was not recognized as such. The fellowship choruses such as "Do Lord," "Say 'Amen,' " "Give Me Oil in My Lamp," and "I've Got the Joy, Joy, Joy, Joy Down in My Heart," were the most contemporary of all Christian songs. They were used in Sunday night fellowships and at camp, but hardly ever in the churches' sanctuaries. In the actual Sunday services the music was a selection of hymns ranging anywhere from 10 to 300 years old. Usually, the "special" music in each week's services was either of a country gospel or operatic nature, depending on the size, geographical area and denomination of the church. Folk music was new and virtually untried.

One of the earliest denominations to utilize modern folk-style music was the Catholic church. The more liberal Catholics were working on the infusion of folk music into the church liturgies. As early as 1964, Ray Repp produced a "folk mass," something completely new to the church scene. Repp's *Mass for Young Americans* was a forerunner of numerous folk masses which would be performed around the nation in a sweep of the Catholic churches. Christian folk records began to come out of the Catholic church also. FEL and Avante Garde were two companies which built up entire lines of Christian folk music recordings.

Youth for Christ (YFC), a Christian teen organization, also had its own spokesman for contemporary Christian music during the early 1960's. He was Thurlow Spurr, who had originally formed a group known as the Spurrlows to minister at a local YFC rally in Winston-Salem, North Carolina.

> Earlier I had heard Fred Waring and the Pennsylvanians in concert, and I was completely knocked out by the beautiful sound of the orchestra and singers. I knew then that I wanted to do something like that except I wanted to do it for the Lord.[1]

It wasn't too much later that Thurlow put the Spurrlows on the road full-time. The work of keeping the group touring led Thurlow to leave YFC in 1960.

The Spurrlows created smooth harmonies and modern arrangements to favorite hymns, traditional songs, and occasionally, new music. As the years progressed, the style of the music they performed paralleled more and more of the current popular styles in secular music. The group developed an increasingly contemporary sound. By the late '60s, they were mixing in rock numbers at a regular rate.

Much of the support for the Spurrlows in the early '60s came from the Chrysler Corporation, which sponsored the group as they toured high schools all over America, promoting drivers' education and safety. They did their Chrysler work in school assemblies by day, and performed both secular and Christian contemporary music in local churches and auditoriums by night. More than a million people heard the Spurrlows each year.

Cam Floria, who worked with Youth for Christ in the Portland, Oregon, area, developed a group very similar to the Spurrlows. Cam's group, the Continentals, developed their own tour patterns, and by the early 1970s they were literally spanning the globe with contemporary Christian music.

The Continentals and the Spurrlows were in reality made up of numerous teams, all using the parent names, each touring different geographic regions in America and abroad. Groups such as the Continentals did much more than just convince adults to listen to pop music styles. They provided training for the singers—not just in performing, but in living in group situations and in relating their faith to others. As one leader described it, the objective was not to be selective in finding the most spiritual and the most professional singers and put them on tour. Ron Bowles, who directed several of the Continental tours, added, "The idea was to enlist those young people who were interested in growing first in their faith, then in their musical proficiency. The singers and musicians in those groups, however, were still above average because of the intense training they went through prior to their tours."

Ron explained why he felt the group experiences were invaluable. "People," he said, "were originally against the idea of contemporary Christian music because they had never heard it performed well. So, they were thinking the *music* was bad rather than the *performers*.

"One of the ways in which the Continentals were an asset was the way they brought quality performance of contemporary Christian music into the church. People were able to see it inside the church and see that it *did* have an effect."

Many of the members of the Spurrlows and the Continentals later went on to form their own local groups. Very often, their concerts were the first taste churches had of anything related to the music of the 1960s and 1970s.

Both Thurlow Spurr and Cam Floria were aided in their endeavors by Ralph Carmichael, who would eventually record both groups on labels which he worked with or owned. Carmichael's crusade to contemporize Christian music had begun as early as 1947.

"Way back then," Carmichael explains, "there was a rhythmic sound that people were listening to on their radios. Just a gentle bass and then a backbeat on the guitar was all there was to it.

"We had music that could be played on keyboards that fit into those tempo slots but the minute you put the bass and guitar and drums with it, and got it to where it was the sound the populace was listening to, then the church folk took exception to it. They would listen to it so long as it wasn't church music, but then they would come to church on Sunday and it had to be just the keyboards again.

"I couldn't figure that out," Carmichael continues, "because I knew that I liked the sound. I loved the strings. I loved the pulse, the rhythms. I didn't understand why we were always having to sing in half notes and quarter notes and whole notes. You could never use the strings, the brass, the woodwinds.''

Carmichael began to search for ways to make those sounds and use them in the Christian field. ''How can you sing about the joy of the Lord,'' he pondered, ''when you can only use the organ or the piano? You couldn't sing about the joy of the Lord using instruments like in the Old Testament—the drums, the cymbals, the sackbut, the stringed instrument, or the loud-sounding brass! It didn't make sense to me! Did God change his mind somewhere between the Old Testament and the New Testament?''

When Carmichael was about 18, his ideas started to develop and his experimentation with sounds began. When he was 21, he organized a band and traveled on holidays.

''We would get thrown out of churches,'' he recalls. ''We had it all there—four trumpets, four trombones, five saxes, rhythm, and sixteen male singers. Things *really* started to happen when we went on television.

''We began to be accepted using strings and a moderate beat, too. There were several years when everything was comfortable because we had fought that battle and they were listening to the strings. I had made an album entitled *102 Strings,* and we were doing big things with big choirs.''

Just when Carmichael had ''won the battle,'' secular music began changing, making a turn toward rock. ''Some musicians made that transition,'' Carmichael adds. ''By that time I had started to do some secular things. I was experimenting and learning my lessons, always hoping that what I learned in the secular field I could bring over and use in the Christian field.

''I didn't like rock. My daughter used to buy rock records and I would break them. I remember the day I went out to my car and I found *her* station on! We developed this 'her' station/'my' station syndrome. She would play the rock and I wouldn't play it. I would play only *my* station. I wouldn't even let her buy rock records with her allowance.

''Then, one day, Roger Williams called and asked, 'Can you write rock?' Well, of course *that* was getting into my pocketbook, so I said 'yes,' and hung up the phone asking myself, 'Why did I say *that?*'

"Roger Williams isn't a rock musician, but things were happening in the commercial field with the influence of rock, so we did a record with a moderate rock beat. It was even eighth notes, if that made it rock.

"The song was 'Born Free' and it was a hit! So my daughter came home from school one day and she had bought 'Born Free' as did about two or three million other people. She flipped the album down and said, 'Is that the same Ralph Carmichael that doesn't like rock?' She had caught me!"

Carmichael continued to experiment. Soon, Billy Graham began production of a film entitled *The Restless Ones,* an evangelistic thrust into the youth scene via film. Carmichael was asked to compose the score. Although by today's standard the music would seem tame, it caused waves among the conservative churchgoers because of its contemporary nature.

"I saw the film and it was so relevant," Carmichael recalls. "The message hit right where people lived. I thought to myself, 'Dear Lord, I hope I can do something more than just the hearts and flowers and the strings and oboe and that kind of thing. Let me do something that really says something to the kids.' So, we went in and we did a score with a fender bass and drum added to everything else. 'In the stars his handiwork I see . . . He's everything to me.' " [2]

The fact that *The Restless Ones* had been produced by the Billy Graham Association tended to ease the worries of the dubious. The film was quite a success at church and youth group showings around the world. The music from the film, especially "He's Everything to Me," is still sung in churches today, many of those churches the same congregations which earlier would not allow it.

Not long after Carmichael had finished the soundtrack of *The Restless Ones* in 1965, Bob Oldenburg, Billy Ray Hearn, Cecil McGee, and a few other cohorts composed the first of at least a score of Christian folk musicals which soon would inundate the churches and religious bookstores of the nation. The first musical was *Good News.*

"What really sparked the idea," recalls Hearn, "was the big movement at that time toward the big road shows like 'Up With People.' We saw a lot of our church kids leaving the church to join up with groups like that.

"So, a bunch of us got together during Recreation Week at the Baptist Assembly in Glorieta, New Mexico, and asked ourselves why we couldn't develop our own 'Up with People' music. We decided to write some music like that by the next annual Recreation Week.

"Meanwhile, we got together a bunch of kids who were there at Glorieta, and some guitars. We started working on some known spirituals and folk songs, and doing some hymns in a folk style. There were about 80 kids, about 20 guitars and a bass, but no drums. *That* was still a little far out."

The youth performed for the Recreation Conference audience in 1966. In 1967, the men completed *Good News,* which was performed for the first time at Glorieta, and shortly after that at the Ridgecrest Baptist Assembly in North Carolina. In 1968, the musical was performed by 1300 young people and a 50-piece orchestra at the Southern Baptist Convention in Houston. From there, *Good News* fever took over.

Kurt Kaiser, a composer who worked at Word Records in Waco, Texas, flew to Houston to see the musical. Kaiser and Hearn then phoned Ralph Carmichael and discussed the possibility of composing more *Good News*-type musicals. All three men saw that music such as that in *Good News* was what the churches *and* the young people needed.

"We discovered that there was a great gulf developing between the youth and the traditional church," Carmichael remembers. "There were very few youth choirs. The church didn't like the kids' music and the church didn't like the way the kids were dressing. They didn't like their hair styles and the gulf was growing wider and wider. The churches were making the kids more and more uncomfortable. There were a lot of influences, but the result was that we decided to try something for the kids."

Carmichael and Kaiser then began writing *Tell It Like It Is*. Billy Ray Hearn moved to Waco and joined the Word staff to promote the musical, and in 1970 *Tell It Like It Is* was released as a record and music folio.

"The gospel was very plain, but the music was those even eighth notes," Carmichael adds. "Different choir directors started to see the potential and youth choirs started growing. One lady who wrote to me said she had two or three kids who would meet with her on

Saturday afternoons. She played *Tell It Like It Is* for them, the kids had become involved in it, and six months later there were 40 kids in the youth choir. This happened over and over. I think we ultimately sold something over a half million of that $2.98 music folio, *Tell It Like It Is.*''

Carmichael and Kaiser then progressed to other musicals, *Natural High* and *I'm Here, God's Here, Now We Can Start.* The two composers gradually pulled away from the "folk" category of the earlier ones and began writing them in a contemporary, quasi-rock style. Not all of the later musicals, however, met with the success of *Good News* and *Tell It Like It Is,* probably for two main reasons. First, the impact of musicals was lessened by a sudden flooding of the market by more and more of the same. Second, many of the follow-up musicals were hastily prepared and too closely resembled their more successful and better predecessors.

Other notable musicals, however, were Otis Skillings' *Life* and *Love,* and Jimmy Owens' *Show Me,* which was performed in the spring of 1971 at Disneyland, as well as in hundreds of churches. Later Jimmy and his wife Carol would team up to write *Come Together, If My People* and *The Witness.*

Composer Owens met with considerable opposition in the late '60s as did the other writers who wanted to introduce contemporary music styles into the church. By 1972, he had found the going somewhat smoother but still difficult.

Said Owens in an interview at that time, "For the first time since right after the Civil War we are able to use contemporary music in the church. All through history there have been periods when the church would for a time speak the language of the people with its music and then the music would become crystallized. The world would continue to grow while the church would hold sacred the styles that had evolved to a certain point. The attitude was like 'If it was good enough for our grandfathers, it's good enough for us. No one can change it. If you change it, you get kicked out.'

"The first guy," Owens continued, "who tried part-singing in church was excommunicated and his soul consigned to hell because they only sang in unison then. I could give example after example all through church history of that type of thing which stems from not being open to the Spirit.

"The Salvation Army Band is a good example. The Army was

founded by General Booth and at the time the brass band was the hottest popular music of the day. Every little town had one, and every little town said 'our brass band is better than your brass band.' You could put a brass band on a street corner and draw a crowd immediately.

"That's what the Salvation Army did because that was the pop style of the day. But, as one Salvation Army Major said to me a few years ago, 'All progress ceased at General Booth's funeral.' Everything crystallized, and anyone who dared change it was changing 'holy tradition' that had come down through General Booth. So the brass band continued on until it was no longer acceptable to the general public. There are still people who love brass bands, but the brass band has become a sort of mockery of the Salvation Army.

"Within the last ten years, there have come up leaders within the Salvation Army who have seen that we have to be bold and we have to change things. If Booth were still alive progress would have continued. It wouldn't have stopped at the brass band. General Booth was a visionary who would have been using rock music by now." [3]

While 1300 Salvation Army units still existed around the country playing the traditional instrumental hymns in 1973, a few rock groups sponsored by the Army began showing up in the midwest and Canada. In England, Joy Strings, a Salvation Army contemporary music group, had released a record album as early as 1965.

According to a February 1973 article in *Right On!*, the few Army rock groups had caused some disgruntlement with the more traditionalistic, old guard members, "who wonder at the merits of using rock music in the salvation of souls." The rock groups were composed of guitarists, an organist, a drummer, five singers and a large brass section (keeping up the family tradition) sending forth the music in the vein of then-popular rock groups Blood, Sweat and Tears, Lighthouse, and Chicago. The article quoted the Army's supervisor of the rock band as saying, "It's not the type of music, but the saving of souls that's important." One Army Major stated, "We've found that direct person-to-person relationships are most effective, and the way to get to the kids is through their music."

Another Army officer working in the New York area recalled General Booth's statement that he "would use the devil's own tune if it would turn one soul out of darkness." [4]

3/

"Jesus Is Just Alright"

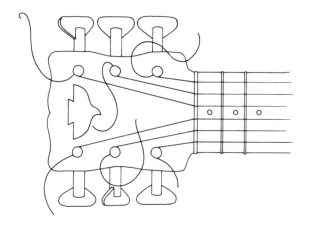

Jesus is just alright with me
Jesus is just alright, oh yeah
Jesus is just alright with me
Jesus is just alright

"HE'S GOT THE WHOLE WORLD IN HIS HANDS." "WHEN THE SAINTS GO Marching In," "There'll Be Peace in the Valley." "There's a Gold Mine in the Sky"; "He"; "Angels in the Sky" and "The Bible Tells Me So."

It may sound like a grand old sermon, but actually it is a list of songs which were popular in the mid- and late 1950s—and not just popular in churches and at camp meetings, either. The songs, recorded by artists such as Pat Boone, Fats Domino, Elvis Presley, and the Crew Cuts (remember the Crew Cuts?), made their way to the top of the secular hit charts.

Popular music of the 1950s was a potpourri of musical styles, ranging from "Sixteen Tons" by Tennessee Ernie Ford and "Around the World" by Mantovani to "Heartbreak Hotel" by Elvis Presley and "Rock Around the Clock" by Bill Haley and his Comets. The variety of pop styles allowed some inspirational or gospel songs to become hits right along with the other pop songs.

In the early 1960s, however, the musical tastes of America began to change. The "war babies," conceived in the years of World War II, had become high school teenagers and would soon be in college. The comfortable, "fabulous fifties" faded, and there began the growing unrest of civil rights inequities, and later a Viet Nam war.

The generation gap widened. Religious sentiments in pop songs faded. From 1961 until 1964, except for Christmas music each December, there were no major pop hits of a religious nature.

In 1964, the nation's music entered a new phase. The music industry was jarred so radically by the Beatles, that in some ways it was as if popular music had just started. The mood was brightened by the British rock, and in the midst of the renewed enthusiasm and hope, pop hits of a religious nature began showing up again. Peter, Paul & Mary made the Top 40 charts with "Go Tell It On the Mountain." The Bachelors sang "I Believe." "You'll Never Walk Alone" was a hit twice in two years, 1964 and 1965.

Also in 1964, the nation was treated to a motion picture starring Sidney Poitier, entitled *Lilies of the Field*. The movie carried a religious theme and featured "Amen," a gospel song written by Jerry Goldsmith. "Amen" quickly caught on as a hit for a soul music group known as the Impressions, and reached #7 on the national hit charts. The Impressions had recorded "Amen" with a march beat rather than a gospel beat. The brass choir in the recording gave the effect of a Salvation Army band, which was many people's idea of what "religion" was supposed to sound like.

In fact, the images of "religious" people and religion in general were an interesting concept. Most people outside of Christianity had been convinced through motion pictures that in order for someone to be "religious," one had to be a mild-mannered, meek priest wearing a clerical collar or a nun dressed in her habit, feeding and caring for orphan children. Even less sympathetic views of preachers were the ranting, raving images presented in *Hawaii* and *Elmer Gantry*. To the Hollywood directors and producers, an average, everyday, level-headed, commonly dressed businessman could in no way represent Christianity or religion.

Thus, the people began believing the images they saw—one extreme or the other, pious or delirious, seldom normal. God was given the image in music of being "the Man upstairs." Seldom was He portrayed as Something or Someone touchable and real. He was nearly always kept aloof. Thus, the religious feelings in pop songs had to be subdued, couched in nebulous terms. Religion was kept cute and harmless, never convicting.

Though the songs weren't always evangelistic, religious music managed to break into the top 20 several times during 1965. The Impressions, hot on the heels of their success with "Amen," recorded "People Get Ready," which reached #14.

Elvis Presley sang "Crying in the Chapel" in 1965, too, and the song smashed all the way to #3. But the top religious hit for the year was the Byrd's recording of "Turn! Turn! Turn!," composer Pete Seeger's paraphrase of Ecclesiastes 3, with certain alterations given to make it a "peace song." "Turn! Turn! Turn!" became the #1 song in America on October 23, 1965.

Then, in the late '60s, another trend in religious pop songs began. Just as the Jesus Movement was drawing people into recognizing Jesus as a personal Savior, the name of Jesus began appearing in pop songs for the first time. Heretofore, song lyrics had referred to God only as "He" or "Him" or "the Lord."

In 1968, Simon and Garfunkel recorded the soundtrack music to a movie entitled *The Graduate*. The most popular song from the film became "Mrs. Robinson," in which this line appeared: "Here's to you, Mrs. Robinson; Jesus loves you more than you will know." [1]

The song was a tongue-in-cheek poke at religion, and was by no means religious, but it was apparently the first time in the rock era the name Jesus actually appeared in a popular song. Ironic that it should take a sarcastic song to open the floodgates of Jesus music!

The ironies didn't end with "Mrs. Robinson" though. In the late '60s, a group of black California high school students, known collectively as the Northern California State Youth Choir, recorded a hymn which was more than 200 years old.

The recording of the hymn was sent to a few radio stations in California, and soon people were calling and asking to hear that "choir" record. A large record company caught wind of what was happening with the song and pressed a new copy of the single for national distribution. To remove some of the religiosity from the group's name (so more pop stations might play their music), the name was changed to the Edwin Hawkins Singers.

"Oh Happy Day" was the hymn. Legend of how the record became a hit says that the song was played as a joke by a rock disc jockey in San Francisco. The joke backfired, and the phones started ringing with requests for it. The superhymn began its stupendous climb all the way to a #4 chart status in June of 1969, and sold over a million copies. The message "Oh Happy Day, when Jesus washed my sins away" was being heard by millions in a popular song.

A two-century-old hymn sung by a black choir had become a top hit in a rock world. Even more ironically, the name of the record company which distributed the first "Jesus hit" was Buddah Records. The popularity of "Oh Happy Day" heralded the start of a long succession of hit songs mentioning Jesus.

Just as a hymn was an unlikely candidate to find its way into the top record charts of the late 1960s, so was a country gospel recording. While "Oh Happy Day" was still selling in stores all over the world, an unknown singer named Lawrence Reynolds recorded a song entitled "Jesus Is a Soul Man." Warner Brothers Records released the single, and it emerged on the national hit charts in September of 1969 and managed to rise to #28 in *Billboard*. Not only was it country music, it was country *gospel* music—unlikely company for the Beatles and the Rolling Stones.

Norman Greenbaum, another newcomer to the charts, was the next artist to use Jesus' name in pop music. "Spirit in the Sky," which first seemed to be a genuine Jesus rock song, was later exposed to be a tongue-in-cheek flay at the Jesus People who were actively witnessing all over the West Coast. Greenbaum told *Hit Parader* magazine, "I wanted to write a thing called a religious song. Jesus Christ is popular and in actuality I used the most popular religious character in my song . . . I'm not a Christian and I don't go to church." [2] Regardless, thousands of young people adopted the hit as a Christian "theme song" during that year. "Spirit in the Sky" became the nation's #3 song in February of 1970.

There were several reasons why songs about Jesus began showing up more and more frequently in 1969 and the early '70s. The Jesus Movement was gaining momentum, and the Jesus theme was a little more acceptable than it had been in years past. Secondly, the youth of the Generation Gap were opening up to *any* possible religion. They were considering each faith's claims and experimenting with each, searching for spiritual fulfillment. To these youth Jesus represented just another religious possibility. Though many of them had turned down the Jesus of their parents, they felt they had discovered a *new* Jesus, with long hair, a beard—so many of the characteristics adopted by the prodigal youth of the late '60s and early '70s. To them, Jesus was a revolutionary.

A third reason for the increasing number of "Jesus" hits was the simple fact that fresh new lyrics were needed as more and more pop songs were vying for hit status. The lyrics seemed to appeal to the masses, so more and more record companies followed the lead set by "Oh Happy Day."

Though not generally recognized by the public as a "Jesus" song, the late 1962 #2 hit of singer Tommy James, "Crystal Blue Persuasion," was written as a result of James's realization of Christ as Savior.

The Youngblood's recording of "Get Together," which had once already been a hit in 1967, returned to the charts in 1969 and reached #5. "Get Together" is one of three "Jesus" hit recordings to become hits in two different years. The other two were Billy Preston's "That's the Way God Planned It" (1969 and 1972), and the questionable "Superstar" (1970 and 1971).

One of the classic albums of Jesus rock music was released in 1970 by Cotillion Records. The album, which unfortunately never reached the hit charts, was *Mylon*, and featured Mylon LeFevre and his band performing a dozen Jesus rock songs. Mylon had been a part of the Gospel Singing LeFevres, a family southern gospel group. He was singing at the early age of five, when, he recalls, he would "stand on the end of a piano bench and face the microphone." He continued to sing with the other LeFevres until he was 25, when his long sideburns and his love for rock music caused a rift.

Mylon had already written songs for Elvis Presley, Merle Haggard, Johnny Cash, Don Gibson, Porter Wagoner, and Mahalia Jackson. Some of the songs became award-winning gospel favorites. But, Mylon wanted to rock. He explained to everyone, upon his resignation from southern gospel music, that he wanted to "reach young people with what I believe in—that Jesus gave His life for my sins—but I'm not gonna shove religion at them."

Mylon's debut rock album contained nearly all Jesus music. His subsequent recordings drifted from the Christian theme, but the first remains an important event in the history of contemporary Christian music.

Ray Stevens, whose "Ahab the Arab" and "Gitarzan" had record buyers assuming that the singer never took things seriously, recorded a song in April of 1970 which turned many heads and sold a million copies. "Everything Is Beautiful" easily reached #1. Although the composition itself was not actually Jesus music, the lyrics told of love for one's fellow man. What put it into the Jesus music category was the children's chorus of "Jesus Loves the Little Children" at the beginning of the recording.

Later that year, the popular Columbia recording group The Byrds released "Jesus Is Just Alright." Though the song was caught up by many Christians, the recording never scored as a big hit. More successful was Pacific Gas & Electric, another popular rock group. Their record, "Are You Ready?," was a powerhouse single that even to this day is not recognized by some as Jesus rock, although the entire content of the lyrics is spiritual and scriptural. The song managed to secure the #14 spot in the nation in the summer of 1970.

The year 1970 was also a banner year for non-Jesus music "inspirational" hits. They were songs which were more or less worldly carbon copies of the trendy Jesus music songs.

Simon & Garfunkel's "Bridge Over Troubled Waters" was wrapped in an ethereal aura and became a hymn for the pop world.

The music was right, the lyrics and recording were stirring; thus, to many people, it was religious. But it was *not* Jesus music.

James Taylor, Johnny Rivers, and R. B. Greaves all reached the Hot 100 in 1970 with Taylor's composition "Fire and Rain." Here, once again, was a borderline case as to whether or not the song was really Jesus music. The song alluded to a definite call for help from Jesus, but Taylor tended to use the word euphonically rather than with conviction. The Taylor version of "Fire and Rain" hit #3 on the charts.

The Jackson 5 produced a stir with "I'll Be There," a song assuring that when everyone else had deserted, "I'll be there to protect you." No one seemed to mind that the singer providing all the reassurance was an adolescent.

Motown Records, who released the Jackson 5 song, also had a #7 hit in 1970 with the Supremes' "Stoned Love." The song passed by many people without their realization that the lyrics in part spoke of God's great love, citing the sun in the sky as a "symbol" of that love.[3]

Much more obvious were the lyrics of "Amazing Grace," an astonishing hit indeed for Judy Collins in 1970. The hymn was written by converted slavetrader John Newton in the second half of the eighteenth century. Collins' #15 recording of "Amazing Grace" was not an updated version, but rather a traditional congregational singing of the hymn.

In 1971, there was hardly a week when at least one "Jesus song" was not on rock radio stations coast to coast. B. J. Thomas sang "Mighty Clouds of Joy." Kenny Rogers and the First Edition even nudged the Hot 100 with another handclapper, "Take My Hand." Rogers, in a personal interview, said he had been influenced by his Baptist upbringing in writing the song. (Several years later, he would make a hit country recording of the hymn "Love Lifted Me"). Johnny Rivers said "Think His Name." Sha Na Na even contributed a parody of all the Jesus hits: "Are you on the Top 40 of your Lordy, Lordy, Lordy?" Ray Stevens revived a 1938 song, "Turn Your Radio On."

One of the most memorable of the 1971 "Jesus songs" was the #2 hit for a Canadian group, Ocean. The song, "Put Your Hand in the Hand," was picked up and recorded by scores of other artists, but Ocean's version stood alone on the charts.

Noel Paul Stookey, on his own as a solo performer following the breakup of Peter, Paul and Mary, made a hit out of a song he had written for Peter Yarrow's wedding. Noel felt so impressed that the Lord had given him the words for "Wedding Song (There Is Love)," he published it under the "Public Domain Fund," and most of the proceeds from royalties for the #24 hit were sent to "The Children's Foundation."

"I assigned the writing and the publishing to them," Stookey said, "because I didn't really feel it belonged to me. I had put up the request before Jesus to write the song for Peter's wedding. It took two or three days for me to get out of the way, but eventually Jesus created the tune. I just wrote it down when it came."

Songs such as "Wedding Song (There Is Love)" and "Amazing Grace" were true Christian songs in the midst of many trendy Jesus songs. At times the dividing line was hard to draw, but in general, the Jesus songs of the late '60s and early '70s were no more than pop songs about a current topic. By 1971, it was nearly impossible to *avoid* hearing mention of Jesus in pop music. For some people it was a pleasant state of the art. Other people had almost had their fill. But the most publicized exploitation of Jesus in the rock music world was just around the corner.

4/

"Jesus Christ, S.R.O. (Standing Room Only)"

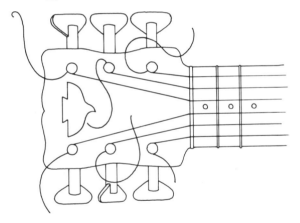

Jesus, you're S.R.O. on Broadway
Told us you'd be back, and what do you know?
AWOPBOPALOOBOPAWOPBAMBOOM
Rolled the stone back from the tomb
And out came Jesus
Starring in a Broadway show . . .

Jesus loves me, this I know
Gave me house seats to his show . . .

JUST AS A CHOIR WAS RESPONSIBLE FOR BRINGING JESUS MUSIC to America's hit charts, a schoolboy's choir was indirectly responsible for what turned into one of the high points in Jesus music's history.

In London, Alan Doggett, Head of the Music Department of Colet Court School, needed a musical piece for his schoolboy choir to sing at their end-of-term concert. Doggett appointed two young British men to compose the appropriate piece.

The result was a fifteen-minute "operetta" entitled *Joseph and the Amazing Technicolor Dreamcoat*, first performed March 1, 1968, at the school by the schoolboy choir. *Joseph and the Amazing Technicolor Dreamcoat* was just what the title implied: a contemporary musical story of Joseph. By incorporating the varying styles of rock and roll, the Joseph story took on new life, and the presentation was a success.

The musical was performed again during the several months following its debut, and by late 1968 it had been lengthened to thirty minutes and recorded. The initial album of *Joseph* was released in England in January of 1969 and, in the words of *Joseph*'s composers, it "received several good reviews but did not set the commercial pop world alight." Copies of the libretto started finding their way into churches and schools in America, but not much more attention was given to it.

By mid-1969, the composers of *Joseph and the Amazing Technicolor Dreamcoat*, Andrew Lloyd Webber and Tim Rice, decided to "have a go at writing something else" since they had been fairly successful with *Joseph*.

Both Webber and Rice had been raised in the Anglican Church, but neither found themselves believing in the deity of Jesus Christ. Rice was to later express to *Time* magazine, "It happens that we don't see Christ as God, but as simply the right man at the right time in the right place." [1] This perspective is most likely what prompted Webber and Rice in 1969 to begin their second work together, one which would view Christ through the eyes of Judas Iscariot, perceiving Christ as a man rather than the Son of God.

The two composers started full steam in that direction. To drum up backing for the musical's completion, the duo composed Judas's theme song, which was also the theme of the opera-to-be: *Jesus Christ Superstar*.

Jesus Christ, Jesus Christ
Who are you? What have you sacrificed?
Jesus Christ Superstar
Do you think you're what they say you are?*

The production of the single record "Superstar" was accomplished in September of 1969, only two months or so after the song had been written. Murray Head was the singer chosen to record "Superstar." Released in late 1969, the recording only reached #74 during the seven weeks it was on the charts.

"Superstar" broke no records at first outing. Its brazen questioning of Christ was too radical for many people. On the surface the record didn't appear to stir much interest in the American public. But John K. Maitland, the newly appointed head of Decca Records, was impressed by the preliminary work on the full opera he had heard and gave the monumental musical a full go-ahead.

And monumental it was. The project called for 18 months of work, 400 hours of studio time, a cast of 11 lead singers, two choirs, six major rock musicians selected from the finest British groups, and a Moog synthesizer. As if that wasn't enough, also employed were the strings of the City of London and an 85-piece orchestra directed by none other than Alan Doggett, who had first commissioned Webber and Rice to write *Joseph and the Amazing Technicolor Dreamcoat*. The man chosen to portray Jesus was Ian Gillan, star of the popular rock group Deep Purple.

Jesus Christ Superstar was tagged a "rock opera," a term which had been first used in billing the highly successful work *Tommy* only a few months earlier. The *Superstar* material was written between October of 1969 and March of 1970, when the recording of the work began. By July the recording was finished, and the historical release date was October 27, 1970.

The 87-minute, two-record rock opera immediately drew publicity from all corners. *The New Yorker* quoted a "major religious leader," Pastor Ralph E. Peterson, as saying "I liked it. It reached me. But the composers are hung up on old-fashioned piety." [2] The writer quoting the pastor said, "Theology-wise, updated, reworked, some nice points, wanders from the book." [3]

Time stated "What Rice and Webber have created is a modern-day passion play that may enrage the devout but ought to intrigue and perhaps inspire the agnostic young." [4] *Newsweek* called the rock opera "Nothing short of brilliant—and reverent. . . ." [5] "A rock opera about the Passion of Christ is a double-barreled provocation. It trespasses on a sublime musical terrain and threatens to profane Western civilization's most sacred religious belief." [6]

From the Christian press came views confirming the prophecies of *Time* and *Newsweek*. Cheryl A. Forbes, in *Christianity Today,* observed that "the wordless finale . . . leaves Christ in the grave. No faith and no victory emerge from this weary music, but the relentless quest remains, haunting and hollow." [7] But Forbes also conceded, "*Superstar* tells what young people are saying." [8]

The *Jesus Christ Superstar* album was sure to be controversial. The shock of hearing a song about Jesus, much more one *questioning* Jesus, was traumatic for many Christians. For others, the recording was a breakthrough—the first time the person of Jesus Christ was put in a "believable" light. Said one observer:

> A common reaction to Superstar is: It was the first time I ever thought of Jesus as a real person. The Phantom-like portrayals of an other worldly Christ on decades of funeral home calendars and Sunday School walls apparently makes the focus on Jesus as a real person a remarkable revelation to this generation.[9]

For some young people, *Superstar* was a crack in the dike of staunch antipopular music feeling within the established church. Not long after the debut of the album, *Superstar* songs were being used in church services all over the country. One theater group, The American Rock Opera Company, managed to perform twenty-two unauthorized performances around the nation before the copyright holders put a halt to the "bootlegging."

By early 1971, talk was beginning about a Broadway presentation of the successful rock opera. Successful, in this case, would be an understatement. According to *Business Week,* "in eight weeks, a touring troupe of about 25 singers and 30 musicians took in more than $2,000,000 in box-office receipts,'' [10] while by October of 1971 the album had sold 3.5 million copies, for a total gross of $40,000,000.

The machines of big business had never before seen so much profit off the man from Galilee. *Time* described it as "the Gold Rush to Golgotha." [11] The title of the rock opera turned out to be prophetic, too. *Newsweek* said that

> the opera makes it natural to see Jesus as a superstar, the new Messiah, who's at "the top of the poll," with Mary Magdalene as chief groupie, Judas as conniving manager, the Apostles his turned-on band, the priests the blind guardians of rigid law and order, Pilate a kind of smooth university president, and Herod, governor of the state. [12]

Opening night at the Mark Hellinger Theatre was the epitome of superstardom for Webber and Rice's Jesus, with advance sales at $1.2 million, one of the largest in Broadway history. People from all sorts of backgrounds attended the theatre to see this man called Jesus to which the marquee in the East had led them. The majority of the people attending loved the show, and the critics generally hated it. The production of Tom O'Horgan (who had also staged the first American rock musical, *Hair*), had turned a fairly acceptable rock opera into a series of "bizarre effects and for-the-shock-of-it images.' [13] *Time* stated "O'Horgan's aim is mainly to shock the sensibilities; often alas, that is all he manages to do." [14]

And then there were the protestors—placard-carrying pickets marching outside the theater, rebelling at the Superstar hat being placed on their King of Kings. The American Jewish Committee issued a seven-page study condemning the anti-Semitic feeling of the play.

Billy Graham wrote in his 1971 book *The Jesus Generation,*

> I don't particularly like the rock opera *Jesus Christ Superstar* because it treats Christ irreverently and perhaps sacrilegiously. But its fatal flaw is that it doesn't go far enough—it leaves Christ in the grave. And without the Resurrection there is no Christianity, no forgiveness, no faith, no hope—nothing but a hoax. [15]

However, a rock music publication later quoted Graham as softening his stand against *Superstar:*

It doesn't mean that they accept Him, but they are taking a new look, because the young can identify with Him. He taught love, peace and forgiveness. He had a beard and long hair. He is seen as a revolutionary in whom they can believe and with whom they can share an experience.[16]

Another writer responded to *Superstar* with this observation:

Pastors who are looking for the record *Jesus Christ Superstar* to make more Christians are going to be greatly disillusioned. A warning is also in order for those who seek after the novel. But, for a look into the souls of men who have confronted the person of Jesus and have not known what to do with Him, *Jesus Christ Superstar* will provide a window. One student remarked that it was too bad that a Christian had not written the contemporary religious sensation. That's right, it is too bad, but then we would not know how the unbeliever feels. Of course, don't get offended by the attitude of confusion of the disciples, the scheming of Judas, the political maneuvering of the priests, etc. This is just the way we all would have acted, if God had placed us in that history instead of the present. I get the impression that the composers would have preferred that Jesus would have never existed. They can't and don't want to believe in Him, but they can't get rid of Him.[17]

Jesus Christ Superstar had its pros and cons, but one thing was for sure: the rock opera, the play and the movie (which was released in the summer of 1973) opened several avenues for Jesus music. In the first place, it came into popularity at the same time the Jesus Movement was reaching its fullest strength. Whether *Superstar* helped the Jesus Movement receive more news coverage, or the national awareness of the Jesus Movement helped draw more crowds to *Superstar* is still open to conjecture. Most likely, each helped the other.

Another avenue opened by *Jesus Christ Superstar* was the financial backing behind it. It would have been a hard task indeed for any Christian body or corporation to utilize the publicity and finances in getting a show off the ground with the same strength and success as MCA managed in promoting *Superstar*. Even though the play nullified the divinity of Christ, it did, as Billy Graham had stated, draw many people to the point of considering Jesus for the first time.

Thirdly, *Jesus Christ Superstar* encouraged struggling contemporary Christian musicians to work harder than ever at producing quality, up-to-date Jesus music. These musicians saw that the public *did* respond to music about Jesus much more than they would have imagined, and who was to say it couldn't happen again, this time from the Christian camp?

Perhaps the hardest pill to swallow for Jesus musicians was the fact that someone in the secular world took the honors for creating mass awareness of Jesus, limited though the perspective was. Encouragement and a challenge, however, came from Cheryl A. Forbes in *Christianity Today* right after the *Superstar* album was first released. "Perhaps," she wrote, "some Christian composer will take the cue and produce a rock opera about Christ that ends not with hollow questions but with triumphant answers." [18]

5/
''Little Country Church''

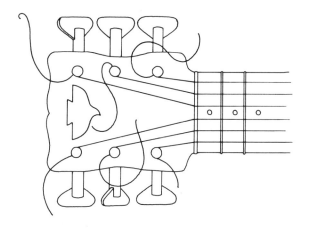

Little country church on the edge of town
Do do do dn do do do do
People coming everywhere from miles around
For meetin's and for Sunday school
And it's very plain to see
It's not the way it used to be
They're talking 'bout revival and the need for love
That little church has come alive
Workin' for each other for the common good
Puttin' all the past aside
Long hair, short hair, some coats and ties
People finally comin' around
Lookin' past the hair and straight into the eyes
People finally comin' around

"Little Country Church" by Chuck Girard and Fred Field.
© 1971 by Dunamis Music, North Hollywood, California 91605. International copyright secured.
Made in U.S.A. All rights reserved. Used by permission.

WITH THE POPULARITY OF JESUS AS THE SUBJECT OF SECULAR
songs increasing in the early 1970s, it would seem that early Jesus
musicians would have had excellent opportunities to have hit
records, too. Such was not the case, however. Most of the songs
which were hits were attempts by secular record companies to cash
in on a fad. Very few stations even auditioned the music on the
religious labels. Secular radio programmers said the music was too
religious while the religious programmers said it was too worldly.
The records of Jesus music performers was either trashed or given
away.

Though the issue against Jesus rock music was a moral one for
many concerned adults, it was far from that for the youth. It was an
excruciating dilemma. Antirock evangelists were stirring up adults
against the Jesus rock, while many of the youth were trying to
explain to their parents that rock music did *not* cause them to fall
into evil habits as the evangelists warned.

Larry Norman wrote the rallying song for the Jesus music fans,
"Why Should the Devil Have All the Good Music?":

I want the people to know
That he saved my soul
But I still like to listen to the radio
They say "rock and roll is wrong
    we'll give you one more chance"
I say I feel so good I got to get up
    and dance

I know what's right I know what's
    wrong, I don't confuse it
All I'm really trying to say is
Why should the devil have
    all the good music
I feel good every day
Cause Jesus is the rock and he
    rolled my blues away.[1]

In the Southern Baptist churches a point well-made by a preacher
would receive a hearty "Amen!" from someone in the audience. In

[1] "Why Should the Devil Have All the Good Music?" copyright © 1973 by Glenwood Music Corporation/Straw Bed Music. Used by permission. All rights reserved.

the world of the 1970s, the musicians became the ministers, and their points well-made in song earned an abundance of "Right-ons!" and plenty of approving applause from thousands of teens.

But the applause often wasn't so much for the performer as it was an outward manifestation of their free expression. Someone was finally saying it as they believed it. When the applause began, Larry would point his index finger upward as if to say "Give God the glory, not me." The teenagers quickly caught on, and the one-way sign became the flag of the Jesus Movement.

> One way, one way to heaven
> Hold up high your hand.
> Follow, free and forgiven,
> Children of the Lamb.[2]

With his long, straight blond hair, his incisive lyrics and his gutsy rock tunes, Larry shocked just about every adult who came into his path. Enigma though he was, he carried the Good News of Jesus via a medium which was readily understood by the young people.

Larry had been playing musical instruments since he was three. His first guitar had been slipped under the bed to hide it from his father. Being a musician was not exactly the most respectable or profitable job in the eyes of his dad, but to Larry it was just about everything.

By the time he was a teen-ager, Larry was singing in his San Jose, California, neighborhood with other musical friends. His band "People" managed a fair degree of success in the Bay Area, and Capitol Records signed them. Their first recording, "Organ Grinder," was not a rousing success, but their second was. "I Love You (But the Words Won't Come)" sailed to the #14 position on the national hit charts in April of 1968.

Larry was already a Christian when the hit came. He was already a bold young man, too, wanting to alert people to the Truth in unorthodox ways. So, he and the band titled their first album *We Need a Whole Lot More of Jesus and A Lot Less Rock and Roll.* But when Larry wanted a picture of Jesus on the cover, Capitol put the

---

[2] "One Way" copyright © 1973 by Glenwood Music Corporation/Straw Bed Music. Used by permission. All rights reserved.

proverbial foot down. It was much too risky and not commercial enough. The LP, with the modified, unimaginative title of *I Love You*, and a photo of "People" on the cover, was released.

On the very same day, Larry broke with the band. Larry went on to do his own creative "thing," doggedly determined not to let "commercial" strictures stifle his creativity and his desire to sing about Jesus.

Only a year or so later, Capitol Records invited Larry back to do a solo album. The result was *Upon This Rock*, one of the first American Jesus rock albums. Though the album never made a hit, it did affect the lives of numerous young people who heard what Larry said in his songs. A good example of those people affected was Kurt Dillinger, then a young Michigan resident.

"I had rebelled severely against my church and its doctrinal teaching," Dillinger recalls. "I had turned to peer pressure, drugs, and similar things in order to be popular. At that time, there was a big Christian movement throughout the United States. Many friends of mine tried to show me that living in Christ was the only way for me to live.

"Music had influenced me greatly as to the direction my life was going, and my idea of *Christian* music was pretty well warped. I thought that to be a Christian you had to fit into the mold that was already set for musicians at that time.

"The people who were leading me to Christ had Larry Norman's album *Upon This Rock*. They had opportunities to share that album with me. I automatically related to Larry Norman, because he seemed to rebel against most Christian music, and was sort of the pilot for Christian rock. Larry seemed to be really speaking a solid message, something that wasn't redundant or being overdone all the time. It was new and refreshing. I don't really think it was the lyrics that got to me as much as the way Norman was free to explain things in his words. They weren't the typical hymn-type songs. I had always thought that music of the Christian world was the hymns or the quartets or some of the music which made me feel like I was going to a funeral every week. Larry's music was lively instead."

I ain't knocking the hymns
Just give me a song that has a beat
I ain't knocking the hymns

Just give me a song that moves my feet
I don't like none of the funeral marches
I ain't dead yet.[3]

"I believe that Larry Norman's album had direct influence on my decision for Christ," Kurt continues. "At that time, I turned about and went directly in the opposite direction that I had been going. After that, his songs encouraged me to bring music into the church, into our youth group. The group grew, and 70 people came to know Jesus. It was because of the freeing power that Christ has, and Larry letting Christ use him through his music."

Upon This Rock wasn't Larry's only Jesus rock album in the early years. Larry produced two albums in 1969 for his own One Way record label, *Street Level* and *Bootleg*. The music on all three of the Norman albums was definitely on the fringe of understanding for adults, but the teens grabbed every word. "Sweet Sweet Song of Salvation," "Right Here in America," "One Way," "Let the Lions Come," "UFO," and "Why Don't You Look Into Jesus" became the bootlegged songs of the Underground Church.

The words of Christ in Luke 17:34–36 concerning the Second Coming were Larry's inspiration to write "I Wish We'd All Been Ready," which would become his most popular Christian song. Unlike most Jesus music, the song was a lamentation.

Life was filled with guns and war
And everyone got trampled on the floor;
I wish we'd all been ready.
Children died; the days grew cold
A piece of bread could buy a bag of gold;
I wish we'd all been ready.
There's no time to change your mind
The Son has come and you've been left behind.[4]

"I Wish We'd All Been Ready" became the anthem of preparation for Christ's return. Teenagers picked up the sorrowful ballad, campfire groups sang it, and soon church youth groups were singing it and trying to teach it to their parents.

A man and wife asleep in bed
She hears a noise and turns her head; he's gone
I wish we'd all been ready
There's no time to change your mind
The Son has come and you've been left behind.[5]

A trademark of the Jesus Movement was the cry "Jesus Is Coming Soon!" Perhaps never since the Apostle Paul's warnings of Christ's imminent return had there been such an electric air of expectancy. Rev. David Wilkerson was sharing his visions and telling congregations that his "bags were packed." Hal Lindsey was shocking the world with his revelations of coming events in *The Late Great Planet Earth.*

The eschatological fervor of the Jesus movement ran especially heavy at Calvary Chapel in Costa Mesa, California. Pastor Chuck Smith, whose Pacific Ocean mass baptisms were given national publicity, formed a new ministerial outreach called Maranatha! Music. The meaning of Maranatha! is "The Lord cometh."

Maranatha! Music released its first album in 1971. *The Everlastin' Living Jesus Music Concert* was an immediate sellout among the Jesus people of California, and numerous copies drifted eastward. Friends mailed other friends copies of the albums, and those who received the records were quick to play them for *their* friends at first chance.

The cover of the *Everlastin' Living Jesus Music Concert* album, which later became known as *Maranatha! 1*, featured the words of Psalm 150:

Praise the Lord! Praise God in His
sanctuary: praise Him in the
Heavens of His power!
Praise Him for His mighty acts; praise
Him according to the abundance of His
greatness. Praise Him with trumpet
sound; praise Him with lute and harp!
Praise Him with tambourine and dance;
praise Him with stringed and wind
instruments. Praise Him with sounding
cymbals: praise Him with loud

---

[5]*Ibid.*

flashing cymbals. Let everything that
has breath praise the Lord! Hallelujah!

Everything in the Jesus Movement years crackled with joy and
exclamation; the true Spirit of the Lord was manifest in the young
people. For the first time in that generation of wars, riots and
tumultuous unrest, the young people were being offered the love
and peace of Jesus on recordings which could be played over and
over, ministering in their own special language.

In the earliest days of Jesus music, there were scattered albums of
folk or rock music which had been recorded by specific groups on
their own labels. The greatest problem for these musicians was
getting their own albums publicized and distributed nationally as
well as locally. Otherwise, thousands of the artists' records were
doomed to their garages and bedrooms.
More than anyone else, Bob Cotterell enabled these musicians to
minister through their records. Bob was a Californian who in 1966
formed Creative Sound, a record production company and distribu-
tor which was responsible for disseminating Jesus music's earliest
albums. Creative Sound's 1972 catalog listed a wide array of
Christian folk music and Jesus rock: *The Everlastin' Living Jesus
Music Concert* and *Come to the Waters*, Maranatha's first two
recordings; *Jesus Power*, one of Jesus music's first sampler albums;
Truth of Truths, a rock opera based on Bible stories; *The
Armageddon Experience*, Campus Crusade's contemporary trouba-
dors; *Jesus People*, a live Jesus music concert; *Soul Session at His
Place*, recorded live at Arthur Blessitt's Sunset Strip club; *Street
Level*, Larry Norman's first album; *Born Twice*, Randy Stonehill's
debut; *Songs from the Savior* from Paul Clark; *Agape*, by the first
hard rock Christian group, and scores of other recordings. Without
Bob's vision, many of the earliest Jesus music recordings would
have never left California.

One of the musical groups on the first Maranatha album was Love
Song. Their music had been a bit more raucous in days past, but by
the time of *The Everlastin' Living Jesus Music Concert*, it had
already become some of the most popular Christian music to be
written in the 1970s.

Love Song's members had met each other through their participation in various other music groups. Jay Truax recalls meeting Chuck Girard for the first time while Jay was working in Salt Lake City as part of the rock group Spirit of Creation. "When I first met him in 1967," Jay recounts, "Chuck had just come from Los Angeles. He'd had a couple of hit records before, like 'Little Honda' with the Hondells and 'Sacred' and 'So This Is Love' with the Castells.

"He'd been singing and playing music for a long time, and I was just playing in night club situations. I had no direction to my music. I was just kinda earning money. We were both wanting a change—a fresh direction in our lives. Some sort of goal."

Jay and Chuck started off together. Not much later a friend of Jay's in Las Vegas had stopped playing music and had gone into full-time study of the Bible. Jay and Chuck responded to the friend's suggestion to "get into the Bible." They left just about everything behind, including old friends.

Jay recalls how people looking for answers and wanting to experience God's love began "accumulating" at their house in Pasadena.

"This is where Love Song came about," added Jay. "It was basically to share God's love. We went into bars and everything. We had some songs about Jesus and about other things. We were radical, man. We'd get kicked out of bars, and no one could even relate to us at that point."

For the next three years they went through all kinds of changes. Chuck read in Luke 18:18–25 the story of the rich man who was told to sell everything he had in order to follow Jesus. Jay and Chuck followed suit, sold everything, and went to Hawaii—the place where they "would never grow old." Their studies of Eastern philosophies became more intense.

"It started out Jesus and the Bible," they recollected, "and our minds took over from there. We never really learned how to walk in the Spirit. We tried to reach up to God instead of having Him reach down to us."

Chuck recalls his stay in Hawaii. "I went to the out-island of Kauai and lived in tents, or anywhere else I could find. I became a sort of 'holy man.' I sat on a rock for five or six weeks, and gradually I began to feel a sense of doing nothing for anybody."

Chuck returned to the States, and while in Las Vegas, was

arrested for possession of LSD. Meanwhile, news had filtered to him about the events and people at Calvary Chapel in California. Chuck finally decided to visit the Chapel. "When I came in that night, it was in the little sanctuary, before they had the big tent. It was a very cozy and warm atmosphere, and the people were all singing praises to God. It was a real feeling of love. I was 26 or 27 by this time, and I wasn't too much into the emotional carryings-on, but I could perceive emotions of a true nature. I was mentally *and* emotionally affected. The whole thing just hit me. I really could feel a genuineness in those people. I felt they really *did* know God. All the other people I'd talked to were always talking about a God that they had to attain, instead of the more personal concept of having Him right now.

"I'd heard about Lonnie Frisbee. He was the hippie preacher there, and I was a little disappointed when Chuck Smith came out to preach that night. Chuck was an older man, but I decided to hear him out. He came out with this big grin and the whole thing was barraging me with images. What is this guy's trip? He doesn't look like the usual guy—the sober thing happening, with a robe and everything! This was more like a mellowed, relaxed atmosphere.

"He just started rapping. It was different. It wasn't like reading a portion from the Bible and then saying a bunch of words. It was like he was sharing someone he knew—Jesus Christ. He wasn't telling me about a God I'd someday find; he was telling me about his personal Friend. He laid all the gospel down." Girard's walls crumbled. He didn't make a decision for Jesus that night, but it wasn't long before he yielded; likewise, Jay Truax, Tom Coomes, and Fred Field. The enthusiasm of these four newborn Christians was hardly containable. As Chuck recalls, almost immediately they composed several songs expressing their faith.

"We didn't have all the right doctrine, but Pastor Chuck and Lonnie liked the songs, and pending a few changes in the lyrics, they invited Love Song to perform at the Chapel. All the gunk went away, and we revamped the lyrics to make them minister."

Love Song's increase in popularity was meteoric from then on. More and more requests for their concerts came into the offices at Calvary Chapel. Their songs "Little Country Church," "Two Hands," "Front Seat, Back Seat," "Maranatha" and others were played and replayed. They drew more and more teenagers to a personal relationship with the Christ who had seemed so unattainable to even Chuck, Jay, Tom, and Fred such a short time before.

With the help of fellow Christian Freddy Piro, Love Song again put their music on record. This time it was a more polished Love Song than had been on Maranatha's first album.

Love Song, the title of their first complete album, was the premiere release on the Good News label. The 1972 record smashed through all kinds of barriers which had been set up around contemporary Christian music. Love Song's album began going places where no Jesus music albums had ever been. In Wichita, Kansas, the album became one of the city's top sellers in the rock record stores. In the Philippines, the title cut "Love Song" became the number one single for the nation—and most of the Filipinos didn't even know Love Song was a religious music group!

In 1973, a seemingly impossible feat was accomplished by Love Song. Four long-haired musicians whose roots were deeply imbedded in rock and roll, had produced an album of Jesus music and had seen their recording become the top religious album of the year.

Love Song went on to record a second album, *Final Touch*, in 1974. The title was appropriate, for the group went on one last national tour and disbanded. The individual members went their own ways, although a few times several of them wound up partners in other music groups.

In addition to Love Song, numerous other young musicians developed at Calvary Chapel in the early '70s: Debby Kerner, Ernie Rettino, Children of the Day, The Way, Country Faith, Karen Lafferty, Good News, Mustard Seed Faith, Blessed Hope, Gentle Faith, Selah, Kenn Gulliksen, and more. The list seemed endless.

In addition to the worship services at Calvary, there were Saturday night concerts held for the young people. The first such concert took place at Milliken High School in Long Beach. Tom Stipe, who ministered at the concerts, recalls those Saturday nights.

"We started holding the concerts," he remembers, "when Calvary Chapel had grown to the size that it needed a new building. Actually, the first few were on Friday, then we moved them to Saturday. A couple of thousand people could be seated in the tent, so we wanted to have the concerts as often as possible. At that time, there was the phenomenon of creativity beginning to take place that was bringing about all of the new California music groups. The Saturday night concert platform in the tent was really a greenhouse for the growth of those groups.''

Rock, folk, and country Jesus music made up only a part of the songs emanating from Calvary Chapel and other such churches and fellowships nationwide. There were the praise songs and Scripture songs, too—simple choruses which either stood by themselves or were drawn from some of the Jesus songs. Karen Lafferty's ''Seek Ye First.'' ''Heavenly Father'' and ''Thy Loving Kindness'' from Lutheran Youth Alive. ''Holy, Holy, Holy'' by Tom Coomes, which he recalls writing after his ''first time through the Book of Revelation.''

Meanwhile, out of the Love Inn community in Freeville, New York, drifted the choruses written by Ted Sandquist—''Lion of Judah,'' ''My Son and My Shield,'' and ''All That I Can Do.'' Pat Terry, along with two Smyrna, Georgia neighbors formed the Pat Terry Group, and wrote ''I Can't Wait,'' a chorus sung around many a campfire before nearly anyone knew who had written it:

I can't wait to see Heaven
And to walk those streets of gold
I can't wait to check into my mansion
And get my sleeping bag unrolled.

Tell me how it's gonna be
Read it from the Bible again
I can't wait to see Jesus
'Cause Jesus is coming again.[6]

Songs came from the Agape Force in California, then Texas. They joined the new simple Scripture choruses going around from town to town as Christians traveled. In a very real sense, the praise choruses and the Scripture choruses were the folk music of the young American Christians.

Tom Coomes, who later became part of Love Song, remembers the impression the Scripture and praise music made upon him the night of his very first visit to Calvary Chapel. "I knew each line even before it was sung. I wasn't used to simple music like this, but it blew me away! It was music which drew people into the Lord's presence! I loved it."

Here was a rock musician, on the eve of being sentenced for a drug charge; a young man who had been to church very few times in his entire life. Yet, here he was, soaking up and enjoying the songs of a most simplistic nature, almost childlike. What was the magic? Both the praise songs (taken from the Jesus music of the day) and the Scripture choruses (simple, easy-to-learn lyrics, often lifted directly from the Bible) were no more than 1970s cousins of the "Singspiration" choruses of the '50s and '60s.

For the most part, people such as Tom, who had never been exposed to Christian fellowship, found the aura of love in the midst of congregational praise an exhilarating if not awesome experience. Their lives in the dog-eat-dog world outside had told them that true *love* was practically unobtainable, and yet they saw and felt love in the songs being sung. All the "press" given to Christianity was contrary to what happened in a service like that! Where was the hellfire and brimstone? Where were the money-grabbing preachers who cared about nothing but taking up the offering? These people were downright enjoying themselves! And look at their hair! It was long! And look at all those bluejeans! This must be heaven!

Facetious though it may sound to someone who has been raised in a true Christian home, this was the revelation of the many young people who found worship in Scripture songs so beautiful; even though in the outside world, their sense of dignity and professional rock music pride would abhor such simple, "emotional" music.

But perhaps the most redeeming feature of the praise music and Scripture music was its ability to draw the two sides of the Generation Gap together. The adults might not like Jesus rock, but they could tolerate and even enjoy the Scripture choruses. The young people had little trouble with the age-old, "antique" Scriptures when they were put to pleasant music which was easy to learn. Because of those reasons and more, praise/Scripture music— even though not unique—was very important in the history of Jesus music. It provided common ground on which the old people and the young people could stand together, as they raised their hands and voices to praise the Lord with "vertical" music. All attention was on the Lord. As one of the popular praise songs said, they were "One in the Spirit" and "One in the Lord."

6/

"Turn Your Radio On"

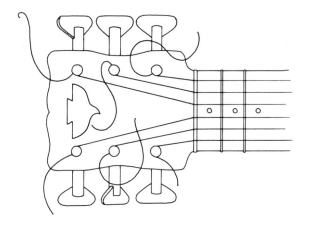

Come and listen to a radio station where the mighty hosts of Heaven sing
Turn your radio on, turn your radio on;
If you want to hear the songs of Zion coming from the land of endless
   spring
Get in touch with God, turn your radio on.

THE GUINESS BOOK OF WORLD RECORDS CITES THE FACT THAT THERE
are more radio broadcasting stations in the United States than in any
other country of the world. In fact, there are more than 8,000,[1]
broadcasting an astounding variety of general and private interest
programming. A study of American radio reveals programs in
languages from Czechoslovak to Navajo, and music from Krishna
chants to disco rock.

Even as late as 1974, of the more than 8,000 stations in the
United States, only 400 to 500 devoted 18 hours or more a week to
religious programming.[2] However, of *that* limited number of
religious stations, not one single station devoted its entire broadcast
day to young people and their music.

Many young Christians had grown up with transistor earplugs as
standard equipment and rock and roll as their language. They were
without one single radio station in the United States which
communicated exclusively to them. If they wanted programs
relative to their Christian faith, they had to tune in to stations
programming music and shows geared either to senior citizens or
grade school children. It was either "churchy music" or kindergar-
ten stories. Very few programs related to teenagers. If those same
Christian youth wanted lively music to which they could relate, the
Top 40 stations were the only answer. Christian programming did
not provide their kind of music.

Unfortunately, there was no happy middle ground for those
young people. They wanted to listen to their favorite kind of music,
but they wanted to sustain their walk with the Lord, too. The
adults—the ones who operated, advertised on, and financially
supported the Christian stations—said "no way" to the forms of
music they misunderstood and literally despised in many cases.
What those often well-meaning adults didn't realize was that by so
dogmatically renouncing rock with "no ifs, ands or buts," they
were giving young people a blatant black or white alternative. Rock
or religion.

The rock choice was a much easier one to make for many youths.
They loved rock, their friends loved rock, and rock was on the radio
in the car, at home, even at school. "Why sit through stale 'shut-in
shows' and 'old fogey' music?" was their opinion.

Meanwhile, non-Christian youth were searching for meaning in their life which they didn't find in church music. The broadcasters, just as much as most church leaders, failed to hear the warnings:

> The church is often represented in our day as hating youth and its smell, sights and sounds. The world of today's culture is exploding with smells, tastes, colors and action which call men to be alive. The church comes from another age and yet is now. This must be so. The message of the Christian faith cannot depend for its essence on the cultural needs of the time. However, the relationship between the faith of the past and the life of the present cannot remain broken if there is to be a living faith.[3]

For many Christian youth, they saw and tasted a music form which was bland and old-fashioned. So, they turned back to rock, and often its evil elements—the suggestive lyrics and psychedelic drug-steeped content.

The youth were wrong to abandon God because his message wasn't couched in their form of media. But there had to be concerned ministers who would step past their own prejudices and realize the immense mission field which existed in the world of rock and roll.

Scott Ross was such a minister, though not in the traditional sense of the word. Ross had an extreme burden to see young people touched with God's love and power. In the late 1960s the young disc jockey, who worked at one of the top rock stations in New York City, became a Christian. His faith and his desire to share it with a lost generation took him in 1967 to the Christian Broadcasting Network in Portsmouth, Virginia, where he attempted to mix contemporary Christian music in with the more traditional records being aired.

Pat Robertson, the head of the Christian Broadcasting Network, recalled meeting Scott at a 1968 Full Gospel Business Men's meeting in Baltimore:

> At the close of the meeting this longhaired, moustached young man came up to speak to me. Despite the fact that he was dressed in a wild psychedelic shirt with tight pants and boots, I liked the sparkle in his eyes and the contagious smile he flashed through his moustache. He introduced himself as Scott Ross and said he was a radio announcer who had accepted Jesus Christ and been baptized in the Holy Spirit just a short time before.

I liked him immediately and later in the summer contacted him asking him if he would like to go to work for us directing programs toward teenagers.[4]

Scott's flashiness and radical ideas caused a considerable stir at CBN. His plans for WXRI-FM, the CBN radio station in Portsmouth, included a gospel rock show. Said Ross:

These dudes on the beach aren't going to listen to the Haven of Rest Quartette when they're groovin' on the Jefferson Airplane and the Beatles. You've gotta start where they are and bring them up to where we are.[5]

It was an uphill struggle all the way. Scott's methods were not well-received. He managed to start his own show, but it just didn't work.

"I went on with a radio program I hoped would reach my contemporaries," Scott later explained. "I tried to play rock music, but the most I could get away with were folk records. I played Peter, Paul & Mary and 'Jesus Met the Woman at the Well,' and all of their songs of that type. Then people would call up and call them 'commies,' and they'd say to get them off the air. It was really, really difficult.

"In August of 1968," Scott continued, "CBN was given five radio stations in upstate New York. I felt the burden for them. Pat Robertson and I had prayed about it, and we felt that I was supposed to go up there and help format those stations. The whole idea was to have a format of deejays on the air playing contemporary music, mixed in with as much good Jesus music as we could find. At that time, that was maybe five albums! We also felt we should speak to the issues out of scriptural perspectives, without coming off as back-to-back preachers.

"Pat thought it was a good concept. He had given me the ball, and I had run with it. They probably were the first radio stations of their type anywhere in the world. We started moving toward it in the fall of 1968, and went on the air in January of 1969."

Before the year was out, troubles began. According to Scott, "Then the Christians started making so much of a hassle that the stations began to back off, because they were afraid of offending the constituency too much and there would be no one to support the station."

Scott recalls that the adults were doing most of the complaining. "The young people were with us! After about four months on the air there, I went to speak at a particular breakfast. I expected to speak to a couple of hundred people and a few thousand people showed up! We did a concert in Syracuse around the same time, and 7,000 people showed up. We were stirring things up. It wasn't just the music. It was the Holy Spirit. The Lord was doing it. People were coming to the Lord in droves. I went on the air with my show early in the evening and sometimes we went on till four or five o'clock in the morning, as an open-ended show. People came to the Lord, phones rang and rang, and we took calls on the air. It was exciting!"

But the hassles continued. Scott and Pat Robertson got together to discuss the situation. Pat, while in South America, had experienced a vision from the Lord concerning a program which Scott could do as a syndicated show. Simultaneously, Scott had also been thinking and praying along the same lines. "Pat really believed in what the Lord had called me to do," Scott remembers. "He literally laid his ministry on the line to give me the opportunity to pursue what the Lord was telling me to do when no one else would allow it."

With Pat's help, "The Scott Ross Show" became the fulfillment of their dream. By early 1970, the show was on sixteen radio stations. The list grew at a rapid pace. Young people were getting their first taste of Jesus music radio, with a show featuring a combination of top secular hits and Jesus rock.

One of his most notable programs in the early days was one in which Scott did a report on *Jesus Christ Superstar*. "There was a show," he recalls, referring to the rock opera and broadway play, "that was unique in itself. It was bringing the Lord right into the midst of the whole music scene. Many people obviously had theological problems with it, but we approached it from the direction that His name is above every other name under heaven and earth: Jesus Christ. Period. You put it on the marquee, and they've got to deal with it, because that's His name.

"We straightened people out as far as the theology of it was concerned, and we had Tim Rice and Andrew Lloyd Webber on the air. It was a powerful segment for 'The Scott Ross Show,' and we made it available to the stations as a religious program."

Meanwhile, Larry Black, who had worked the afternoon shift on the CBN New York network, went on the road selling "The Scott

Ross Show," which within several years would be broadcast on 175 stations nationwide—the most extensive syndicated contemporary Christian show in America.

The year 1970 was the premiere year of another nationally syndicated Jesus music show, the year I began broadcasting "A Joyful Noise." The dream of broadcasting a show of Christian pop music had been born while I worked with chapel youth groups in the service overseas. I had found a few songs which alluded to God, such as "Hymn" and "Tramp on the Street" on Peter, Paul & Mary's *Late Again* album, and was excited about the possibility that there might be more songs of that type.

As soon as I returned home from the service, I began visiting record sections of department stores, scavenging for any Christian folk or rock music I could find. In April, I contacted a friend who worked for a rock and roll station in the Tampa area, where I lived. I asked him if he would assist me in producing a sample show in which I would feature the best pop songs about God I could find.

We both found it an exciting prospect. The first step was getting the records to play. At the radio station where my friend worked, there were two giant cardboard boxes full of "trash" records—the hundreds of 45 singles which WFSO chose not to broadcast. They were generally saved to give away as contest prizes. For me, they were much more important than any contest prize I could ever win. I hoped there would be a few God-oriented records amongst the boxloads, because they were just what I needed.

The search went on for hours. Each title of each song was scrutinized for any reference, direct or indirect, to God. Surprisingly, they began showing up. "Good Morning, God," "Streets of Gold"—they weren't "biggies" like the smash hits they were playing in the radio studio one door down, but who cared? They were building a repertoire for my first show! "Down on My Knees," "God Grows His Own"—likely and unlikely titles from a stack of rock records.

Then I picked up two Capitol singles which were in a stack together. The first was by Pat Boone, entitled "Now I'm Saved," and the second was one by a singer named Larry Norman, entitled "Sweet Sweet Song of Salvation." Pretty bold Christian titles for pop records on a label such as Capitol!

I ran into the production room and reviewed each likely candidate I found. By the time I got to Larry Norman, I knew I had latched onto something. Never before had I heard such a raspy, rock and roll, and totally unchurchy voice singing such an obviously Christian song. As heretical as my reasoning would seem to some people, I knew I had found just the right ingredients of a shocking new form of Christian radio!

I was anxious to record my first show with these records no one had wanted. I put them with the hit Jesus songs I already had; "Jesus Is a Soul Man," "Jesus Is Just Alright," "Oh Happy Day," and a few others, and recorded the first show.

In the true spirit of a rock and roll disc jockey I wanted to shock everyone. Not in a negative way, but in a way which would open everyone's eyes to the reality that there *could* be dynamic rock music about the Maker. I had searched the Scriptures for references which might be appropriate for beginning the show. In that study I found more than thirty references in the Bible which entreat us to "make a joyful noise unto the Lord." With rock music we had the *noise*, what was missing was the *joy!*

Psalm 95:1 was my choice for the opening. "Make a joyful noise unto the rock of our Salvation." I read the verse in a straight tone, fully expecting half the rock and roller listeners to cry "yuk" and reach for the radio knob. But what came next was the shocker. With a wailing guitar and crashing drum came a rock version of "The Lord's Prayer" (one of those giveaway singles), and "A Joyful Noise" had already lived up to its title.

Through the help of Herb Hunt at rock radio station WLCY in St. Petersburg, "A Joyful Noise" hit the air on a Sunday morning only a few weeks later. The first all-Jesus rock radio show, featuring nothing but songs about the Lord and His teachings, was a reality.

Other rock stations got word of the show. Residents of Wichita, Oklahoma City, Denver, Nashville, Richmond and Indianapolis were soon hearing Jesus rock music on their favorite rock stations each Sunday morning. There were so few records at the start, each week I would play many of the same ones rotating them into a different order to make the show sound fresh. For a while, "A Joyful Noise" featured the top 10 Jesus music records each week, only because there *were* only 10 Jesus music records.

Any discussion of pioneer Jesus music radio should include the early broadcasting ventures of people such as Scott Campbell. Scott began a show of contemporary Christian music in 1968 on KARI in Blaine, Washington. KARI was a Christian station, and Scott recalls, "I played everything I could get my hands on that was good, contemporary Christian music."

In other areas around the U.S., other innovative Christian deejays and programmers such as Scott began playing as much contemporary music as the station managers would allow. Some of them often sat through long lectures in the manager's offices for their enthusiastic updating of the standard musical fare. Others were just plain fired.

A sad irony developed. Religious station programmers, unsure of rock music, avoided nearly all of it, regardless of lyrical content. Rock station programmers, hardly concerned about the harmful effects of rock music, turned out to be some of the first broadcasters of Jesus music, via the Jesus rock of popular performers and the authentic Jesus music on syndicated shows such as "A Joyful Noise" and "The Scott Ross Show."

As was traditional, the church fell one step behind by not opening itself more to the question of whether rock could be an efficient medium of the Gospel. It would be 1975 before the first all-Jesus music radio station would hit the air.

7/

"Day by Day"

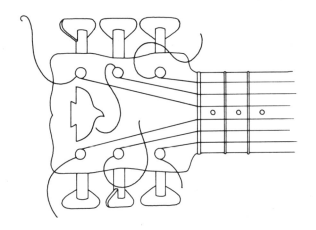

Day by day, day by day
Oh, dear Lord, three things I pray:
To see thee more clearly, love thee more dearly,
Follow thee more nearly, day by day.

—*Stephan Schwartz*

THE MOVIE THEATER WE SAT IN WAS ONLY HALF-FILLED. THE FILM we were about to see wasn't a box office smash as the off-Broadway play had been. But my two friends and I were excited at the prospect of viewing any "religious" film which truthfully put Bible stories on the screen.

The city streets of Manhattan, bustling with shoppers and crowds, was the unlikely setting for the film. Soon, a ram's horn was heard and the strains of "Prepare Ye the Way of the Lord" emerged from the crowded streets. The fantasy began. The New York City residents who were to be the main characters of the film threw away their earthly woes and possessions and joined the singer. The din of street noise faded away as the characters danced and sang their way into the land of Godspell.

With the fantasy begun, a young white man with an afro-type hairdo appeared. He wore overalls and a Superman T-shirt. His face was painted as a clown's. He was Jesus, being baptized by John in a New York fountain.

I was totally caught up in *Godspell*. Because of the allegorical style, I was taken offguard, but I was excited regardless. My two friends, however, weren't quite so pleased. After only a few moments, they left the theater.

When I saw my friends the next day, I inquired about their leaving after only about ten minutes. They explained that both of them had been offended by the sacrilegious tone of the film. It made fun of Christ by putting him in a clown suit. They didn't want to see what happened next.

As far as I was concerned, I was entertained and at times edified by *Godspell*. I would see the film nearly a dozen times in the next five years, something of a record for me. Each time I was refreshed.

The differing views that day in the theater were indicative of the opinions being voiced everywhere. *Godspell* had been conceived and directed by John Michael Tebelak; the music had been written by Stephen Schwartz. Based on the Gospel according to St. Matthew, the play was a musical review done in what one magazine described as a mixture of "slapstick, vaudeville, satire, circus and expository preaching." [1]

The difference in *Godspell*'s stage presentation and that of *Jesus Christ Superstar* was extensive. *Superstar* had portrayed Christ in a flashy, superstar role; *Godspell* showed him as a gentle clown. *Life* magazine's theater critic Tom Prideaux stated that "compared to *Jesus Christ Superstar*, *Godspell* is a carefree beggar beside a rich Pharisee." [2] A more humorous comparison was that offered by *The Christian Century*: "*Godspell*'s ho-ho Jesus and *Superstar*'s woe-woe Jesus." [3]

Superstar had never allowed the resurrection of Christ, and *Godspell* left the resurrection "just offstage." The hornets' nest stirred up by *Superstar* among the more conservative Christian population was still buzzing when *Godspell* appeared on the scene. Tebelak's portrayal of Christ as a harlequin was just as offensive to the conservatives as the deluded Jesus in *Superstar*.

What the critics censured was what the supporters applauded—a characterization of Christ as a humble and gentle leader, teaching his followers to be as little children and always to look to him for answers. He directed them with love and wisdom so simple it was profound. The play brought to life Matthew 18:4, in which Jesus said "Except ye be converted, and become as little children, ye shall not enter into the kingdom of heaven." The clown figure of Jesus allowed the plain message of the Gospel of St. Matthew to come through loud and clear, not just in words, but also in acted-out parables.

Director Tebelak, who had conceived *Godspell* while working on his master's thesis at Carnegie Tech's School of Drama, stated, "The church has become so down and pessimistic. It has to reclaim its joy and hope. I see *Godspell* as a celebration of life." [4]

And a celebration it was. Stephen Schwartz composed the music and wrote new lyrics for *Godspell*. Several of the songs were Anglican hymns and anthems of yore, with new musical foundations constructed by Schwartz. According to one report, "when asked how he could give such fresh tunes to old hymns, Schwartz said it was no problem at all since he had never heard the old tunes." [5]

Schwartz's songs in the play ranged the entire gamut from rock to barroom music, each song taking on the character of the scene in which it was used. The song which rose out of *Godspell* as the greatest commercial hit was "Day by Day," one of the revitalized hymns Schwartz used. "Day by Day" reached the #13 position in national pop music charts in May of 1972.

In 1973, the movie version of *Godspell* came along, following record-breaking runs for the play in places such as the Ford Theater in Washington, D.C. The movie was greeted with the same span of opinions as the play had been.

Certain Christian publications, such as *Christianity Today*, gave the *Godspell* film positive reviews. However, some other critics flayed at the film for presenting a too-shallow view of Jesus and an overall too-shallow play, (even though the script was lifted almost directly from a 2000-year-old literary masterpiece). One disappointed writer went so far as to describe *Godspell* as "the Gospel according to St. Cutesy-poo." [6]

Though such critics tore down the play and the film, and though many people were greatly offended by the unholiness of *Godspell*, lives were affected. To some people the actors may have portrayed "cutesy-poo" characters, but to many the play was much more significant.

Scott Ross, whose wife Nedra sang for several years as part of the pop group The Ronettes, saw *Godspell* do some heavy work. "A well-known secular record producer called Nedra and me one day," he recalls, "and asked us to come to New York City and see *Godspell*, because he wanted Nedra to record a couple of songs from *Godspell* for a secular label. I'd already seen the show, but we took up the invitation and went to New York to see it with him.

"We got to the end of the show where the Lord is crucified on the chain link fence. All of a sudden, this producer, who knows nothing about the Lord to my knowledge, grabbed my hand. I turned and looked, and he had grabbed Nedra's hand on the other side. He had sunglasses on, but I saw the tears streaming down his face. I'm not overdramatizing the instance—the tears were literally streaming down his face. I could not believe it, because I knew something about this guy's life. He trembled. He shook from head to foot.

"I looked around in the audience, and I'd say half of them were Jews, people in show business. It was a new show, everybody in town was trying to see it. People all over the auditorium were crying. This friend we were with couldn't take it any longer. He jumped up and ran out the door.

"After the end, when the cast had come down the aisle saying

'God is not dead,' we went outside and our friend was standing on the sidewalk. He said, 'We've got to go eat something.' He was still trembling. He said, 'Tell me about Jesus.'

"We sat for five hours in his apartment telling him about the Lord. He didn't ever make a commitment, nor did Nedra ever record that album, but I know that that day something happened in his life. A seed was planted in a major way."

Though Godspell's producer Tebelak said he did not consider his play a part of the Jesus Movement, it was. There was no way of avoiding it. The same young people who had expressed their joy in Christ in and out of churches gladly embraced a chance to experience that joy in the theaters of the nation, too. To them, *Godspell* was an excellent alternative form of entertainment.

Photo Section:

1. Early Concert Bill, 1967
2. The Start of Maranatha's Weekly Concerts, 1971
3. Singer-Songwriter John Fischer, 1970
   Credit: F. E. L. Records
4. Pioneer Jesus Music Deejay Scott Ross
   Photo courtesy of Love Inn
5. The Love Inn Barn, Freeville, New York
   Photo courtesy of Love Inn
6. Jesus Rock Group Agape in Concert— California—(circa 1973)
   Photo courtesy of Agape
7. Calvary Chapel in its tent days—Costa Mesa, California (1973)
   Photo courtesy of Contemporary Christian Music
8. Praise gathering at the beach, Pastor Chuck Smith of Calvary Chapel is on right—California Coast (1972)
   Photo courtesy of Contemporary Christian Music
9. California Jesus music group Harvest Flight on stage (early 70's)
   Photo courtesy of Gary & Debbie Cowan

Noble Productions Present...

THE TEEN·SCENE

ONLY 1800 SEATS

ALL SEATS $2.00 DONATION

The "Now Sound" of Gospel Music
Featuring

THE NOBLEMEN
Fresh - Contemporary - Exciting

*

Andre Crouch & THE DISCIPLES
Soul Music from the Heart

*

THE VELVETONES
Velvety Smooth, Modern Blendings

*

Chas. McPheeters & THE NEW CREATURES

Singing Great, Original Gospel Folk Music

*

EMBASSY AUDITORIUM
847 S. Grand St. - Downtown Los Angeles

Sat. Night - Nov. 11 - 8:00

*

FOR TICKETS | CALL (213) 547-3264 • 832 - 2788 • 773 - 7410
or Send *$2.00* Per Ticket to Nobel Productions
807 West 10th Street * San Pedro *90731*

(All proceeds to Southern Calif. Teen Challenge)

1

10. Phoenix Sonshine performing (early 70's)
    Photo courtesy of Gary & Debbie Cowan
11. Ernie Rettino & Mike MacIntosh (1971) Long Beach Sports Arena—California
    Credit: Greg Wigler
12. Denver coffeehouse of the Holy Ghost Repair Service, Inc.
    Credit: Charles McPheeters
13. Love Song concert at Lee Park in Dallas during Explo '72
    Credit: Ron Smith
14. Nearly 200,000 concertgoers attend Explo '72 Finale in downtown Dallas (1972)
    Credit: Ron Smith

15. Woodall Rogers Parkway—Wall-to-wall people in downtown Dallas, Explo '72
    Credit: Ron Smith

16. Paul Baker Making a Joyful Noise in Wichita (1973)
    Credit: Kevin Bilderback

17. Malcolm & Alwyn—two of Jesus music's British imports
    Publicity photo

18. Andraé Crouch and the Disciples on the NBC-TV "Tonight Show"
    Publicity photo

19. Larry Norman at KDTX-FM Studios-Dallas (1973)
    Credit: Stoney Burns

20. Ron Salisbury & the J. C. Power Outlet (circa 1973)
    Publicity photo

21. Terry Talbot performing at Praise '74, Costa Mesa, California
    Credit: Paul Baker

22. The Road Home Celebration, in a Colorado Springs rodeo arena. Pikes Peak is in the background (1975)
    Photo by Paul Rey

23. Debby Kerner, one of Maranatha's first recording artists
   Credit: Greg Wigler

24. Billy Ray Hearn directing orchestra for Honeyfree performance, Road Home Celebration, Colorado
   Springs, (1975)
   Photo by Paul Rey

25. The New Christy Minstrels in the mid 1960's. Barry McGuire is the third man from the top.
   Publicity photo

26. Barry McGuire—1975
   Photo by Paul Rey

27. The Castells in the mid-1960's. Chuck Girard is the third from the left.
   Publicity photo

28. Chuck Girard at Fishnet '76. Front Royal, Virginia
   Credit: Paul Baker

29. Wing and A Prayer at Knott's Berry Farm. (1974)
   Credit: Dan Aguilian

27

28

29

30. The Road Home. (1974)
    Credit: Tom Stipe

31. Randy Matthews. Myrrh Records' first Jesus music artist.
    Dharma Artist Agency publicity photo

32. The 2nd Chapter of Acts praising the Lord at 1975 Colorado concert.
    Photo by Paul Rey

33. Mike Johnson, whose Jesus music days started in 1967 with the Exkursions.
    Dharma Artist Agency publicity photo

34. Songwriter/musician Pat Terry. (1976)
    Credit: Paul Baker

35. Terry Talbot, Randy Stonehill, Larry Norman, John Michael Talbot, Paul Baker, at 1st FCCM National
    Conference, Angola, Indiana (1976)
    Credit: Paul Baker

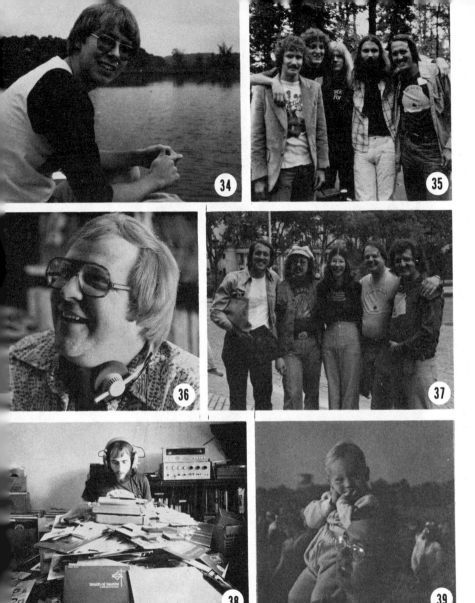

Deejay Larry Black, host of "The Larry Black Show"
Photo courtesy of Larry Black

Contemporary Christian communications personified; Paul Baker, deejay; Mike Warnke, comedian; Honeytree, musician; Lou Hancherick, publisher of Harmony; and Danny Taylor, musician. Pittsburgh, Pennsylvania (1976)
Credit: Paul Baker

One of the world's "champion" Jesus music cataloguers and collectors, Dan Hickling, in Buffalo (circa 1977).
Credit: Steve Lipman—Buffalo Jewish Review

"Raising them in the nurture and the admonition of the Lord . . ." Scene at Jesus '76, Mercer, Pennsylvania
Credit: Paul Baker

40. Jesus '77, Agape Farm, Central Pennsylvania.
    Credit: Paul Baker

41. "Raised in the Newness of Life . . ." Water baptism of hundreds, Jesus '77, rural Pennsylvania.
    Credit: Paul Baker

42. The "Covenant Woman"—Janny Grine (1976)
    Credit: Greg Wigler

43. Maranatha group Children of the Day (1976) Riverside, California
    Credit: Greg Wigler

44. Jesus '78, Near Disneyworld, Florida. White speckles in center of photo are blankets spread on
    ground in front of stage.
    Credit: Paul Baker

45. Steve Camp, Amy Grant and Marty McCall, backstage at KBRN Lakeside Park concert, Denver,
    Colorado (1978)
    Credit (Paul Baker

46. Pat Boone and daughter Debby, (1978)
    Lamb & Lion Records Publicity photo

47. Jesus rock group Petra at Wichita Jesus Festival of Joy (1978)
    Credit: Paul Baker

48. The Resurrection Band, part of Jesus People, USA. 1978 FCCM National Conference, Lindale, Texas
    Credit: Greg Wigler

49

50

51

49. Daniel Amos and their many hats. 1978 FCCM National Conference, Lindale, Texas . . .
Credit: Greg Wigler

50. . . . They have many spectacles, too.
Photo courtesy of Contemporary Christian Music

51. At the end of a very important lunch, the beginning of new understanding. Danny Taylor, Bob Larson, Paul Baker and Tom Stipe. Denver, 1978.
Credit: Kathy Larson

52. The nation's foremost contemporary Christian communicators, during a broadcasters' seminar in Denver, Colorado (1978)
Front Row: Dan Johnson, Word, Inc.; Evie, Word recording artist; Don Perry, personal manager for B. J. Thomas; Keith Whipple, KBRN; Dan Lienart, Good New Records; Rick Painter, KQLH; Rob Dean, Word, Inc.; Jerry Bryant, "Jesus-Solid Rock"; Arnie McClatchey, KYMS; Roland Lundy, Word, Inc.; Chris Christian, Myrrh recording artist.
2nd Row: Johnny Lowrance, Word, Inc.; Larry Black, "The Larry Black Show"; Steve Horton, New Pax Records; David Benware, David Benware & Associates; Jim Lawson, KCFO; Paul Porter, KLQB; Rich Germaine. KGDN/KBIQ; Laurie de Young, WYGR; Benton White, WWGM.
3rd Row: John Duffy, KLYT; Dan Hickling, Word, Inc.; Dough Corbin, Lamb & Lion Records; John Styll, Contemporary Christian Music; B. J. Thomas, Myrrh recording artist, Jerry Thomas, brother of B. J.; Paul Stillwell, Twelve Oaks Productions; Mike Trout, Twelve Oaks Productions; Dave Michaels. WPIT-FM; Paul Baker, "A Joyful Noise"; Tim Mathre, KAIM.
Credit: Chris Swallow

WALKING IN JESUS LOVE

Jesus Loves You Denver

HE'S ALIVE !!

Jesus '76
July 1, 2 & 3 Charlotte, North Carolina

EST '73
AUGUST 9-11, 1973

LARRY NORMAN

Jesus '78 ORLANDO FLORIDA!
APRIL 6, 7 & 8

ADMISSION
...day, August 7
...ewood Bowl

'78
July 27, 28, 29

A three-day outdoor celebration of faith and ministry unto the Lord!
It's gonna be great at Fishnet '78!

GOOD NEWS CELEBRATION

INCLUDING A NEW YEAR'S EVE MESSAGE BY PASTOR CHUCK SMITH, OF CALVARY CHAPEL IN COSTA MESA

TUESDAY, DECEMBER 31, 1974
6 P.M. to 1 A.M.

KNOTT'S BERRY FARM

I found it KM...

WORLD TOU...

THE SALT Co. PRESE...
SALT FESTIVAL

...3, 14 & 15, 1978
...ROYAL, VIRGINIA
...hnet '78

JULY 27-29
'78

...AMPING, TEACHING, OUTREACH

AUG. 1, 2, 3   MERCER, PA.

MERCER BARN

JESUS

JESUS MUSIC EVERY NIGHT
A JOYFUL NO...
PAUL BAKER KDIX-FM 102.9 10P...

One Nat...
Under G...

8/

"Pass It On"

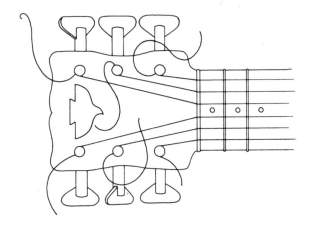

PASS IT ON by Kurt Kaiser

It only takes a spark to get a fire going,
And soon all those around can warm up in its glowing;
That's how it is with God's love;
Once you've experienced it;
You spread His love to everyone;
You want to Pass It On.

JUNE 1972. THE TEXAS SUN SEEMED TO BE A LITTLE HOTTER THAN USUAL. Texans were used to their share of sunshine, but the drought conditions of the recent few months had farmers praying for badly needed rain. It wasn't to a crucial stage yet, but the drought was causing concern.

In 1972, residents of Dallas were still living down the city's reputation of being the place where a President of the United States had been gunned down nine years earlier. Dallas Cowboy fever was somewhat a diversion as the football team became world champions of the Super Bowl in Miami earlier that year.

As early as 1971, hints had been dropped that "something historic" was going to happen in the "Big D" Dallas in June of 1972. Newspapers started to divulge more about what was being planned. Billboards announced the week of June 17–22 as that historic week-to-come, the week when an estimated 100,000 young people would converge on Dallas to participate in Explo '72, the Student Congress on Evangelism.

The man behind the plan for Explo '72 was Bill Bright. In 1951, Bright, then owner of Bright's California Confections, founded Campus Crusade for Christ. Campus Crusade was to the churches of America what the Jesus Movement had been to street people. Much more organized than the spontaneous Jesus Movement, Crusade people had worked aggressively at winning college-aged and high school-aged students to Jesus with the help of many churches. Bright's goal was to see by 1980 global saturation of the gospel—to see all nations have the opportunity to hear the Good News. Explo '72, the World Student Congress on Evangelism, was part of that goal.

Using the techniques and publicity methods he knew as a businessman, Bright orchestrated the gigantic congress, to be attended by representatives of all 50 states and nearly 100 countries. Mailers announcing Explo went out to all regional Campus Crusade offices nationwide—and the word began spreading.

Finally, in early June, teenagers, college-aged youths and older adults began the pilgrimage to Dallas. Explo '72 bumper stickers decorated cars and luggage from Washington to Maine, and much farther. All the cars headed toward Texas.

Finally, the week of Explo came. Dallas had never seen such an onslaught of young people. All airplanes into the airport were filled. Motels were packed with wall-to-wall teenagers. Backyards of private residences were turned into campgrounds as Dallas area residents extended a welcome to the Explo crowds. A tent city was built at an RV campground near Dallas, and the rows of tents and campers seemed endless.

Although there were teaching sessions going on throughout Dallas each day as part of Explo, the main gathering place for the multitudes was the Cotton Bowl. Each night as many as 80,000 delegates poured into the giant stadium for preaching and music. The preaching came from Billy Graham and other renowned speakers, and the music came from the widest array of musicians ever to gather to worship the Lord at one time.

The Cotton Bowl meetings were far from typical. Cheers pierced the warm Texas air: "Gimme a J! Gimme an E! Gimme an S! Gimme a U! Gimme an S! What've you got? Jesus!" The people in the crowd—a lot of them, at least—had Jesus, and much more. They had an enthusiasm which made the older guests rejoice and shudder at the same time. The young might be returning to active life in the church—but did they have to be *so* enthusiastic? Even when a full-fledged thunderstorm dumped tons of water on the Cotton Bowl crowd, the cheers turned to roars of applause for each clap of thunder provided from the heavens. As one student commented, "Almost 80,000 people here in the Cotton Bowl prayed that it wouldn't rain tonight. There were probably about 200,000 farmers praying that it would. We were simply out-voted." [1]

One of the climaxes of Explo '72 was the candlelight service held toward the end of the week, when the estimated 80,000 people in the Cotton Bowl lit candles in a "Great Commission" service. As each person lit the candle of a person next to him, the entire stadium sparkled with the beautiful light. The people sang "Pass It On," written by Kurt Kaiser as a part of the 1970 musical *Tell It Like It Is*.

Kurt remembers that night well. He was watching the television coverage of Explo from a motel room in Cincinnati. "It was probably one of the most moving experiences of my life. I never would have imagined that one simple song would go so far. But I'm so very glad it was used in that way!"

Explo '72 was a major step by the churches not only to bring back their prodigal youth, but also to re-fire the enthusiasm of church youth. The established church leaders trusted Campus Crusade more than the less-defined Jesus Movement in the streets, which they often viewed as drawing the young people *away* from the church.

But Explo '72 was historic in another way. Noteworthy were the numerous concerts of gospel music presented at the Cotton Bowl each night, at various parks and churches throughout the week, and on the Woodall Rogers Parkway the concluding day.

The day-long concert near downtown Dallas drew 180,000 Christian *and* non-Christian people to hear the most varied program of gospel music in America's history. The program of performers and speakers that sultry June day was overwhelming: Billy Graham, Johnny Cash, Randy Matthews, Larry Norman, Danny Lee and the Children of Truth, Katie Hanley (star of the Broadway production of *Godspell*), country singer Connie Smith, Andraé Crouch and the Disciples, Willa Dorsey, the Armageddon Experience, Reba Rambo, Barry McGuire, Vonda Kay Van Dyke (former Miss America), The Speer Family, and many others, including an appearance by Kris Kristofferson and Rita Coolidge.

Gospel music would never be the same again. The music programs at Explo '72 gave every visiting delegate a chance to pick a favorite style of gospel music, and take home word of what had been heard. For several music groups and solo musicians, Explo '72 was their springboard to national prominence.

In fact, just a few months later, several of the musicians who had performed at Explo were in Madison Square Garden for a Labor Day concert. "Jesus Joy: A Solid Rock Gathering at the Garden" featured Love Song, Danny Lee and the Children of Truth, Katie Hanley, Lillian Parker, and the Maranatha Band. Speakers included Tom Skinner, Scott Ross, Fr. Jack Sutton, Moishe Rosen ("Jews for Jesus"), Bob Mumford, Charlie Rizzo, and Jerry Davis (editor of New York's Jesus paper, *Good News of Jesus*).

"Jesus Joy" concerts provided the same opportunity of worship for northeasterners as had the Maranatha concerts in California and Explo in Texas. In Carnegie Hall, "Jesus Joy" had sponsored a concert a few months prior to Explo featuring Andraé Crouch and the Disciples and Danny Taylor. The crowd at Carnegie Hall overflowed into a Baptist Church across the street. While Danny performed in the Hall, Andraé Crouch and the Disciples performed at the church. Then, while everything was "cooking," the performers switched stages and did the whole concert again. What could have turned into mayhem, turned into "Jesus Joy ." Both Danny and Andraé recorded the Madison Square Garden concerts for albums. Danny's was released on Tempo Records and Andraé's on Light.

Andraé Crouch and the Disciples were rapidly becoming the best known gospel group in America. Andraé had made giant strides in contemporizing gospel music, and he took much flak for doing so. Critics lambasted his rock interpretation of the gospel, but soul gospel music was Andraé's life and the beat didn't bother him at all. "It's the rhythm of the heart," he'd say.

Andraé began playing piano as a mere child, and was raised in a church environment which made gospel music second nature to him. In 1965, he brought together a few friends to form a singing group known as the Disciples. The Disciples stayed with Andraé through several years of work at Teen Challenge in Los Angeles.

In 1970, however, Andraé Crouch and the Disciples became a full-time ministry. The group recorded a single, "Christian People," which hit the secular charts in some locales after its release on Liberty records.

The next step was a recording contract with Light records, and Ralph Carmichael "adopted" them to *Take The Message Everywhere*. Andraé's music was quickly taken up by young people, especially songs like "I've Got Confidence," "Through It All," "I Don't Know Why (Jesus Loved Me)," "Bless His Holy Name," and "My Tribute (To God Be the Glory)."

Andraé's enthusiasm while performing was infectious; likewise, the Disciples'. They even accomplished the "impossible" by appearing on the "Johnny Carson 'Tonight' Show" (he introduced him as Andrew Crouch). By that time, the Disciples were made up of Bili Thedford, Sandra Crouch (Andraé's twin sister), and Perry Morgan. Backing up Andraé on the show was a group known as Sonlight, who themselves had recorded an album for Light records. Sonlight included Fletch Wiley, Bill Maxwell, Harlan Rogers and Hadley Hockensmith.

By 1972, the songs of Andraé were beginning to be accepted by older Christians as well as the youth. Andraé Crouch and the Disciples' appearance at Explo '72 just reassured that acceptance. The hands clapped. The feet stomped. The people sang and praised the Lord with one of the men most responsible for the growth of Jesus music.

Because of the growing response of audiences to the music such as that which Andraé Crouch and the Disciples played, Word, Incorporated in Waco, Texas, was watching ever more closely for new contemporary Christian talent. At the time of Explo '72, Word was rapidly approaching prominence as the largest religious record publisher in the world.

Word, Inc. was founded by Baylor University graduate Jarrell McCracken in 1953. In the mid-1960s, Word and Ralph Carmichael's Light Records, a division of Word, had been instrumental in modernizing Christian music. Records by The Spurrlows, The Continentals, The Jimmy Owens Singers, Ralph Carmichael, and Andraé Crouch and the Disciples paved the way in the recording industry for Jesus music.

As Word focused more and more attention on the new Christian music, the Myrrh label was established, with Billy Ray Hearn coordinating the production of albums by Ray Hildebrand, Randy Matthews, Dove, and a few of Thurlow Spurr's contemporary groups, such as Dust and First Gear.

Both Ray Hildebrand and Randy Matthews had done an album on the Word label before the formation of Myrrh. In 1962 and 1963, Ray had been "Paul" of Paul and Paula, whose recording "Hey Hey Paula" had sold close to 3,000,000 copies. Ray had written the song during the summer between his junior and senior year at Howard Payne College in Brownwood, Texas, where he was an all-star basketball player. When it was time for recording the song, the scheduled singer didn't show up. So, Ray did the singing with "Paula," and within a few months, he was on the road all over the world for a straight year and a half.

When he returned to Texas, Ray was soured. "I was tired of chasing around the world after something that I wasn't even sure I wanted," he said. "I had recorded a hit album, but the royalties were slipping off. I couldn't see devoting my life to dirty jokes and night clubs. What for?

"That's when I started reading the Bible again. I had been raised in a Christian family, but I had never really asked the real questions about life or my faith. That's when I realized the Good Lord was trying to teach me something."

So, Ray signed with Word Records for two albums. Then, he

moved to the new Myrrh label and recorded a third LP. Ray's greatest contribution to Jesus music, however, was his 1967 album, *He's Everything to Me.* The songs from that album were circulated among many churches who had previously not been open to contemporary music.

Randy Matthews was a bit more the radical than Ray. He was no stranger to rock music—his father Monty had helped form Elvis Presley's first backup group, the Jordanaires. But Randy took the rock music one step further. "I reached an age where I had to rebel from my father," Randy related. "I sang acid rock until those guttural, animalistic noises nearly ruined the quality of my voice. The band did very well. But I never wrote anything until I found Christ."

After his senior year in high school, Randy joined a gospel group called the Revelations. Though the Revelations were a gospel quartet, Randy somehow always managed to inject rock into what they were singing. The Revelations toured for two years, while Randy also attended Ozark Bible College. He then moved to Ohio to attend Cincinnati Bible Seminary, where his music took a turn to street ministry. He helped organize "The Jesus House" in Cincinnati, where 250 young people attended weekly.

During his Cincinnati days, Randy recorded his first album, *Wish We'd All Been Ready*, on Word records. The album was quite radical for its time, and it had very few contemporary counterparts on the Word labels. In fact, Randy was the first Jesus rock solo artist at Word. As soon as Myrrh records had been formed to capacitate the contemporary musicians, Randy was a natural for the first album.

All I Am Is What You See, Randy's first Myrrh album, was a collection of excellent Jesus music songs, many of which became his most popular: "Johnny," "Sunny Day," "Country Faith," and "Time To Pray." Randy moved to Nashville, and took up residence as one of the east coast's best-known Jesus music performers.

The work wasn't glamorous by any means, though. On a live album released in 1975, *Now Do You Understand?*, Randy told his concert audience,

It was about four years ago now that I started traveling around the country playing my music for God. Back then they called it "gospel rock and roll.'' There wasn't a lot of places to play "gospel rock and roll.'' You couldn't play in churches; they were afraid you'd rock and roll them out of the pews. You couldn't play in colleges 'cause they were afraid that you would sell "prayer picks" after the concert. So I was left to play mostly where I could, and that was on the street payin' some dues and learning' some lessons.

I learned a lot of important things living on the street like that—and goin' without food. I learned that materialistic things, they just all pass away. They're of no value really at all. I also learned that for those of us that love the Lord, everything works together for the good, even though you can't see it at the time.

Another lesson that I learned was that dill pickles can be a great comfort to you. You can buy a five-gallon jar of dill pickles really cheap, man. What you do is get it and put it in the trunk of your car, and when you get hungry you open up that five-gallon jar of dill pickles, stick your hand down in the pickle juice, and you take out one, big, green, warm dill pickle. After you've eaten one of those, you don't want to eat for a couple of days anyway.[2]

Dill pickles in jars, sardines and pork and beans right out of the can cold, and Kool-Aid to wash it down. They might have been unusual fare for most people; but for the Jesus musicians, it was part of "payin' the dues."

9/

"Fat City"

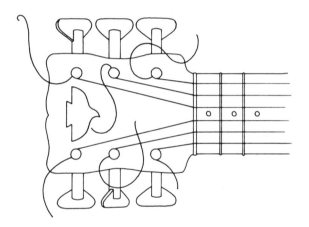

Fat City,
I could be livin' in.
In Fat City. I could be sittin' real pretty.
But it wouldn't mean a thing without you.
I could be a millionaire and the master of my time,
But if it wasn't spent with you, it wouldn't be worth
   a dime.
I could know all there is to know about that glorious
   fame,
If you went and left me, life would never be the same.
No, it would never be the same without you.

TOURING IS WHAT KEPT MOST OF THE JESUS MUSICIANS GOING. THE lack of contemporary radio, national record distribution, and church acceptance had ostracized them from the normal church "circuits" enjoyed by the larger, more "established" music groups. While many of these other musicians sat before giant church suppers and home-cooked meals, the Jesus music troubador often ate what food was left in the trunk of his car. Concerts came so few and far between. The work hardly kept the artist alive. Some solved the problem by taking on part-time jobs; others just stuck it out.

Tom Stipe, who worked with the groups out of Calvary Chapel, observed, "If you go physically seven days or so without a good night's sleep and good meals, you will get sick. Our groups would come back from almost every tour with well over half the band sick with colds and the things that were related to the lack of proper nutrition."

Tom recalls one of the groups going to a certain area for a series of concerts, and it had not been communicated that the sponsor was to provide meals for the group. "The group literally went two days without food," he added, "because they were broke and they felt embarrassed to bring the subject up to the sponsor.

"Probably the hardest things to take in the early days of touring," Tom explains, "were misunderstandings and the problems of growth. In one group I was in, there was a situation where we'd stay in hotels; the expenses were all included and we'd just take care of ourselves on the road. But there's a whole other world in which 90 percent of the Christian groups—and in the early days 99 percent—would fall into. That was where you would go out on the road in your van, or maybe a trailer. You wouldn't be flying all your stuff in fancy flight cases. You'd be just touring. You'd drive into a town and you'd be at the mercy of your sponsor.

"Sometimes you'd walk into a situation where the people would be absolutely ready for you. But in the early days, we found that it was really hard to communicate to people the physical needs in a touring situation. When I say physical needs, I don't mean physical *luxuries*, because hardly anyone expects luxuries on the road. But sometimes you'd walk into a situation and ask . . . 'How about blankets and a pillow?' They'd say, 'Blankets and a pillow? I thought hippies slept on the floor.' Then they'd say, "I didn't know there were seven of you. I thought there was just a soloist in this group!'

"Now, I've heard of some groups who go in and insist on a feather mattress and a certain kind of pillow. That's absurd. There's some people that spend their whole time complaining about everything, but that's not the element that I'm talking about. I'm just talking about those early days when people were beginning to relate to the spiritual and physical needs on both sides—the sponsor and the group. Sometimes there was a complete lack of communication.

"Some sponsors had the idea that the communication was done simply by the name of the group. In other words, 'Well hey! These guys, they have a record out, they must be famous. We'll just spread it around a little bit.'

"So you come into a town and no one shows up at the concert. The people go tell the artist, 'I thought you'd fill up this auditorium.'

"You start asking questions. You ask them, 'How many fliers did you make up?'

" 'Well, just a few because we thought you guys were famous. We thought you'd draw in the unbelievers.'

"You start quizzing a person on how much work and prayer have gone into a situation and they really kind of expected that your presence there and your name would somehow do the evangelism for them. They never communicated things like what street the auditorium was on, what time the concert was, what type of concert, and who was playing.

"Then there were the spiritual preparations; communicating to the body of Christ as a whole just what was going to be expected spiritually. There used to be a lot of gaps upon coming into a town and finding there was no prayer, or there had been disunity in the church. In many cases we'd walk into situations and find that just the planning of our concert had created great divisions in churches."

The early years of touring presented trials for the wives and girlfriends of the musicians, too. In some cases, the wives toured with their husbands. But often, it was a matter of enduring at home. Tom's wife, Mary Ellen, recalls those days:

"The times that I remember were as a girlfriend when Tom was on the road. I recall the heartbreak of watching the poverty they went through in those early days—memories of them coming home from the road after being gone for two weeks with no money and then living on macaroni and cheese for a week. The girlfriends kept trying somehow to supplement the guys' incomes by bringing over meals or pinning $5 bills to their door screens or whatever we could do to get them through.

"In those days, Tom would rarely call me on the phone when he was touring because of the expense. So, I mostly got letters. I can remember, too, my friendship with the different girls in Love Song, and I recall watching them go through it as they struggled financially. I often wondered then if I really wanted to marry someone who was in the music ministry. But I did. And when it came my turn, it was basically a time of learning how to get through it!

"What do you do when your husband is gone for three weeks and leaves you alone? There were other girls who had my similar problem, so what we would do was stay in the same house and share food bills. That would give us fellowship spiritually, and also someone to talk to. We weren't so lonely and we could share financial resources as well.

"We'd pick out whoever had the biggest house and just all go over there, kids included. The guys didn't normally always call on the same night so it was really neat to stay with the other girls. One of the other girl's husbands would call and we'd have word of all of them—what they were doing and what was happening on the road. That way we interspersed the phone calling, too, and it wasn't so long between calls. You could find out what your loved one was doing from the other one's husband.

"I remember times when the guys would call us and they'd tell us that they'd had a bad gig and we'd get depressed for them. We'd share the agony and get in a circle and pray. As wives, that was the main thing that we were called to do when the guys were gone. If we were at all in the Spirit, as Christian wives it was our duty to pray. So, when they'd call and there would be a bummer, we'd pray and at times we'd think, 'Is it worth it?'

"The hardest thing for me to take would be when people weren't appreciating the talents my husband had to share, or if they belittled him in some manner. For instance, a lot of people think that the preaching ministry has some kind of supremacy over the ministry in music. Tom used to get criticized especially for his music ministry—since he has both callings—to choose music above preaching. Some people would think that was really a drag. Yet, I believed in him and I believed in his music ministry. So it used to be hard for me when people would come down on him as a musician or not understand his calling. That would be the hardest thing for me to have to handle—the hardest thing to give to the Lord. But in most cases we'd come to the Lord in prayer and He'd take it from us.

"A lot of times, wives, friends of mine and I would go to gigs and we'd have to sit in the audience and listen to remarks from straight church members coming down on our husbands for their songs or for what they were doing. Those people had a complete misunderstanding of the musicians' calling and, at a lot of places, since we were sitting next to those people, we would be the ones who would have to take up the banner and explain to them what contemporary Christian music was all about.

"It was such a pioneering spirit involved, the whole family had to be behind it. If the wife wasn't behind him in the early days of the Christian music scene, I don't know how a man ever made it. If his wife was nagging at him to get out of the music ministry along with all the other pressures involved with just being accepted, there was no way he could ever get through."

One wife who actually worked on the road with her husband was Karen Johnson. Mike and Karen performed on stage together. Though Karen says the two of them usually had enough to eat, she remembers most "not having a place to go home to."

For the Johnsons—Mike, Karen, their dog Jessie, and later a baby son—home was a small trailer they pulled behind their car. At nights they parked it in driveways, truck stops, roadside rest areas—"anywhere we could put it," Mike recalls. The Johnsons lived "on the road" for several years before they finally moved into a "real, honest-to-goodness *home*" in Nashville.

As hard as touring is, doing concerts is often much easier and less risky for artists or groups than investing hundreds or thousands of dollars in an album which may or may not wind up in their garages in unopened cases.

There were quite a few Jesus musicians and groups who never even got to the stage of having a record album, but were very much a part of spreading the word through contemporary music. Since no albums were recorded, the only legacy they left was in the changed hearts of those who heard and heeded their musical message of Christ.

One of the most common faults in the music world as fans is the haste to assume that when no record album is released by an artist, or when there is a lull in between record releases, that means the artist is either backslidden, a has-been, or in an unfruitful ministry. Though any or all of these can be true, musicians sometimes feel that their concert ministries are much more important than a record.

Also, there are some musicians who simply sound much better on stage than on record, more humorous in person than recorded, and generally minister more effectively face-to-face with the audience. In some of these cases, a recording and the time involved to make it would be a diversion from the Lord's intended work in their lives.

Hundreds of small, hometown bands and solo artists with no recordings helped to keep the fire smoldering during 1973 and 1974, the "Underground Years."

10/

"It's Only Right"

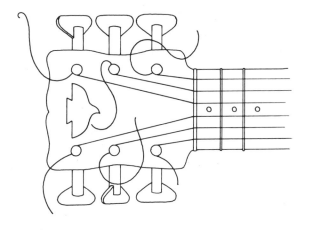

Traveling with a three-man band
Singing every place I can
I got a burning desire to sing my song
I used to be a lonely girl
Living in a lonely world
But everything changed when Jesus came along
It's only right I should be singing
Because the Holy Spirit's bringing
A little more joy, a little more love into my heart
  each day
No matter where the Spirit leads
You know I'm gonna trust and obey
And keep singing this song all along the way

"ONE WAY INN," "JESUS CHRIST POWERHOUSE" "THE FIRE Escape," and "The Belly of the Whale," are just a small sampling of the descriptive names given to Christian coffeehouses in the Jesus Movement years and after. Sometimes the coffeehouses were small and quaint. But usually, they were no more than a rented-out storefront. The interior decoration was colorful Jesus posters or even wall murals; the carpeting was a patchwork of old carpet sample squares in a rainbow of colors. There was usually a coffee machine and a Coke machine off to one side, and there was a good chance the sponsors of the coffee house would set up a small "Jesus People" bookstore, with contemporary Christian books and records, gospel tracts, bumper stickers, T-shirts, and miscellaneous items.

Christian coffeehouses were spin-offs of the 1950s beatnik rendezvous in New York and elsewhere. Some served particular purposes, such as the coffeehouse founded by the Christian World Liberation Front in the Haight-Ashbury district of San Francisco in 1967. It provided a place of retreat for students and other youth during tumultuous times on Berkeley's campus.

Further down the California coast, in Hollywood, "The Salt Company" was started around 1968 by Don Williams, college pastor at Hollywood's First Presbyterian Church. The coffeehouse was especially noteworthy because it was supported by an "establishment" church. In those days, such an affiliation was rare. The Salt Company was first located on the church premises, but about two years later was moved to a more ideal location for witnessing—across from Hollywood High School. A music group, also named The Salt Company, was formed to minister at the coffeehouse and elsewhere.

Also, in Hollywood, Arthur Blessitt's "His Place" on Sunset Strip presented an alternative to the scores of topless clubs and bars which surrounded it. "At 'His Place,' " Blessitt explains, "we had some Jesus music performed there, but we didn't promote that. 'His Place' was called a Gospel Night Club, but really all we had was a piano, a stage, and people bringing their instruments and playing. We had free coffee and Kool-Aid, and we were open all night. You couldn't sleep there overnight, but you could get free food, clothes, music, and preaching at midnight.

"We did not feature rock music in 'His Place,' because there were all of these other clubs, bamm, bamm, bamm down the Strip. We had crowds filling our building, lining the streets when there wasn't even any music. They wanted to come in for something that was casual, where some guy over here was just plunking at the piano or somebody over here strumming a guitar."

One of the musicians who performed at "His Place" was Charles McPheeters. Charles had been through an almost unbelievable life of drugs, the occult, "and the whole general mess," he recalls. His travels took him from California to Seattle in 1965, where he began to minister in a trio known as the Disciples Three. "Even then," Charles remembers, "our folk style drew opposition from many church people who seemed to like their traditional type music more than what we were doing."

Charles had gradually worked his way southward—through the Berkeley "Filthy Speech Movement," as he called it, into Los Angeles to work with the Southern California Teen Challenge Center, where Andraé Crouch was directing a forty-voice addicts' choir. Charles changed his trio's name to the New Creatures (there was already a music group working with Andraé known as the Disciples), and moved to work with Arthur Blessitt at "His Place."

Arthur recalls an extraordinary night at the club which served to show the important role of the Christian coffeehouses and clubs. "The sign on the front of our building said 'His Place,' " Arthur explained, "and it looked like an old bar dive. Charles McPheeters and the New Creatures were playing. This guy came walking down the street and heard the music. He was bar hopping and popping pills and he saw 'His Place.' So, he walked in loaded and sat down on the floor. The guy looked up and saw Charles. He said, 'Brother!' It turns out that this guy was Charles' brother, Jim, who had just come back from Viet Nam.

"Charles didn't even recognize his brother. Charles had been converted, but Jim hadn't.

"Jim had been through the same stuff Charles had been through—the drug scene and all. He had joined the Marines, gone to Viet Nam and come back. Charles didn't even know about his return to the United States!

"Anyway, Jim came in and sat down. He listened to Charles, but he didn't even know he was a Christian. There he was just playing gospel music! So, when he finished, Jim came up, and boy, they hugged!

"Later we both talked to Jim and shared with him the love of Jesus. He didn't receive the Lord that night at 'His Place,' but the next morning he went to church with Charles, prayed, and gave his heart to Christ. Jim then started working with us, moved into our halfway house on weekends, and joined my staff."

Ultimately, Jim McPheeters, O. J. Peterson and a couple of other men formed a group called Eternal Rush, who performed at Blessitt's club and traveled with him on his famous cross-country cross-carrying walks. "His Place" stayed open until 1972. "Then," explains Arthur, "we became a tourist attraction. The Jesus Movement thing exploded and whammo! We were just inundated with tourists."

Charles McPheeters traveled extensively after leaving "His Place." He went to New York with his wife Judy and for a while lived with the people at what would later be called "Love Inn." During the summer of 1969, Charles worked a stint as midday deejay on the CBN network of stations.

By 1972, Charles migrated west again, but only as far as Denver, Colorado. There, he became a Youth Pastor at Redeemer Temple, and ultimately formed a youth ministry known as "The Holy Ghost Repair Service, Inc." Working with Redeemer Temple as a missionary outreach of the church, this ministry rented a couple of store fronts and opened a coffeehouse/counseling center on East Colfax Avenue. Part of the Holy Ghost Repair Service's ministry was an underground newspaper, *The End Times.*

Coffeehouses served the Christian and non-Christian youth alike. While they were missions to the wandering street people, they were also gathering places for Christian young people who found them a pleasant alternative to other forms of entertainment and fellowship. If the leaders of coffeehouses handled the operation of such houses properly, the Christian youths, after visiting several times, would be thrust into a responsibility of witnessing to the down-and-out youths, the runaways, and the drug addicts who sought solace in the coffeehouses. In many cases, the houses were the only mission work to which the Christian young people were exposed. Thus, they were places of Christian growth as well as rebirth.

Hundreds of coffeehouses appeared and disappeared, the casualties often due to lack of financial or community support, lack of proper leadership, or a lack of vision. There are still coffeehouses existent, frequently out of the mainstream of church activity, and often receiving very little attention from anyone outside the ministries. Because the mission work to drug-hooked teens and runaways is not a glamorous job, the work goes on virtually underground.

Numerous of these Christian coffeehouses around the nation provided places for the young Jesus musicians to perform. Not only were they extremely important conduits for the new tunes of the day, these houses also provided excellent training grounds for the musicians: "The Avalon" in Akron, Ohio, "The Greater Life Coffeehouse" in Dallas, "The Salt Company" in Detroit, and hundreds of others.

Notable as a starting ground for several musicians was "The Adam's Apple" in Fort Wayne, Indiana. The coffeehouse, sponsored by Calvary Temple, actually began in a tent, and director John Lloyd recalls that his first concerts featured non-Christian rock bands in order to draw a large number of young people. But some of them didn't stay non-Christian for long: John's preaching and ministry reached the musicians, too, and several of them accepted Christ through the very ministry they had played for.

The "coffeehouse" eventually moved inside a building, and the crowds filled it weekly. Soon, "The Adam's Apple" was known throughout the midwest for its concerts. A few of the best-known Jesus music artists of the decade began their ministries at "The Adam's Apple." Among them were Petra and Nancy Henigbaum.

Nancy had sung in non-Christian coffeehouses several years before she came to Fort Wayne. "My first coffeehouse job," she recalls, "seemed like the pinnacle of success at the time. I started hanging around with older people and doing things I thought 'mature' people did: smoking, drinking and doing dope. I thought I really knew what life was all about. But I must have made an amusing picture—a teenage girl with braces on her teeth, singing 'I'm a mean, mean woman.' I was actually quite naive and fragile."

Nancy described her life style as "rejector of conventional society—in other words, freak." Her friends began to call her "Honeytree" when they found out it was the literal translation of her German name. She and her friends experimented with astrology, tarot cards, mind-expanding drugs, eastern religions, utopian fantasies, current movements, and "everything unusual."

It was this curiosity concerning the sciences and religion that drew her to investigate Calvary Temple in Fort Wayne while she was there visiting her sister. While at the church, she met John Lloyd, whom she heard had at one time been into drugs himself. The next day, Honeytree visited with John, which resulted in her acceptance of Jesus as Savior.

As a young Christian, Honeytree tried to "live the life" but finally succumbed to drugs again. "Then it seemed like the Lord picked me up by the scruff of the neck and landed me in Fort Wayne again," she remembers. "By this time John and the other Christians had started a coffeehouse called 'The Adam's Apple.' I found myself working in the midst of those friendly Christian freaks, happier than I had ever been before. That was when I realized that Jesus had not left me at all. He was just teaching me a lesson. I learned that joy comes from working for Jesus and being around other people who are working for Jesus, too. After I learned that, I never got stoned again.

"John started dragging me everywhere to sing and give my testimony. Eventually, I ended up being John's secretary, working full-time for 'The Adam's Apple,' and doing musical programs on weekends. God had always impressed on me that if it weren't for the Adam's Apple and the church that got the whole thing started, I would still be a confused Jesus freak, getting high to feel spiritually alive, instead of doing something fruitful with my life."

Honeytree began her recording career with *Honeytree*, recorded on a custom label, later picked up by Myrrh Records in 1973. Her excellent songwriting talents brought forth songs such as "Clean Before My Lord," "I Don't Have to Worry," and "Heaven's Gonna Be a Blast."

Calvary Temple in Fort Wayne and the "Adam's Apple" are good examples of the interaction that was possible between church and street ministries, and between churches and the Jesus musicians. Of course, Calvary Chapel in Costa Mesa was another. Out of the Peninsula Bible Church in Palo Alto, California, came support for the ministries of John Fischer and Pam Mark (Hall). Both John and Pam were "products" of the Discovery Art Guild, encouraged by Peninsula Bible Church.

In Nashville, the Belmont Church of Christ sponsored the Koinonia Coffeehouse. The coffeehouse, across the street from the church, provided a platform for top Jesus music groups and artists such as Dogwood. Belmont proved to be the worship place for many musicians, including singer/writer Gary S. Paxton, who admits he "sat outside the church, across the street, watching for several weeks to see what the people were like" before he went in. Going to church was a brand new experience for Paxton. He had several million-selling records to his credit—but a destroyed life was all he had to show for it.

In Van Nuys, California, a part of the Greater Los Angeles area, the Foursquare "Church on the Way" was yet another center of worship and spawning ground of young Christian talent. Pat Boone and his family, Jimmy Owens and his family (including daughter Jamie), and the Wards—Matthew and Nellie, with their sister Annie and her husband Buck Herring—all worshiped at the Church on the Way at various times throughout the years of the Jesus Movement.

Out of those three families alone came more than a dozen albums of contemporary Christian music, including several musicals. The Boone family recorded for Word, then Lamb & Lion Records. Jimmy and Carol Owens wrote and recorded their musicals for Light records; their daughter Jamie recorded her first album on Light in 1973, entitled *Laughter in Your Soul*. The 2nd Chapter of Acts (Annie, Nellie and Matthew) did backup vocals for many of these recordings before doing their first album, *With Footnotes*, in 1974.

Included on the 2nd Chapter's album was a short two-minute, 20-second song entitled "Easter Song." Written by Annie, the song almost immediately caught on as the "Hallelujah Chorus" of the Jesus Movement generation.

Hear the bells ringing,
they're singing that we can
be born again.*

Within weeks the song was learned by thousands of people, and by the time the 2nd Chapter of Acts passed through a town on tour, nearly half the audience sang along.

Joy to the world!
He is risen!
Hallelujah!*

The jubilation of "Easter Song" pierced through the hardest hearts, and people rose to their feet whenever it was performed on stage.

The 2nd Chapter of Acts, in addition to recording their own album, began touring and singing in concerts across the country. The charisma they exuded onstage quickly captured the audiences, and joy was usually the trademark of a 2nd Chapter concert. Annie, her husband Buck (who produced the group's albums and worked the sound in their concerts), Nellie and Matthew became the ambassadors of contemporary Christian music during the "Underground Years" of 1973 and 1974. Their music not only ministered to thousands of impressionable youth; it also introduced Jesus music to church leaders and congregations who were still reluctant to accept the new music into the church.

The 2nd Chapter's music wasn't usually hard rock. Granted, there were certain songs which Matthew would belt out Stevie Wonder-style, but the majority of the music was the unlikely combination of light rock tunes and hymnlike harmonies. Though Annie wrote contemporary music, the classical feel of the songs permitted adults to enjoy it as much as the youth. The 2nd Chapter was one of the very few Jesus music groups whose music was unique—it did not have a parallel in pop music.

Then there was Barry McGuire, a former pipe-fitter who probably came as close as anyone except the Beatles and Elvis Presley to changing America with a single song.

In 1960, Barry borrowed a guitar from a friend and taught himself some of the more popular folk songs of the day. It wasn't too long before friends invited Barry and his guitar to parties. The next step was singing nights away in bars for $20 and tips, and Barry loved it. But the moonlighting took its toll on the singing pipe-fitter. He finally laid down the tools and joined a few friends in forming the New Christy Minstrels.

---

* "Easter Song" by Anne Herring. © 1964 Latter Rain Music (ASCAP) Used by permission.

For the next four years, the New Christy Minstrels were one of the top singing groups in the world. Their performances of hits such as "Green Green" and "Saturday Night" were held at such prestigious places as the White House, Carnegie Hall, Coconut Grove, the Hollywood Bowl. They also sang in Hawaii and Europe. The New Christy Minstrels were the first American recording group to have a commercial release in Russia.

"We did one-nighters for four years," Barry explains. "Friends I called would ask me, 'Where are you?' and I'd answer, 'I don't know, but the area code is 316.'"

Barry was around some of the richest people in the world—senators, heiresses, entertainers—but he noticed over and over that none of them were really happy. They were more bored than anything else.

The happy minstrel became a soured cynic. He became disillusioned, and started losing respect for the people around him, including his audiences. He began to peruse books on the sciences—biology, neurology, and psychology—"trying to find out why we think and how we think." Those studies carried him deeper into the mystical sciences, existential thought, and studies of the power of the mind. Barry had always heard that "the Truth will set you free," and he continued to search for that Truth.

In 1965, after his breakup with the New Christy Minstrels, Barry recorded "Eve of Destruction." In spite of its banishment from numerous top radio stations in the country because of its stinging controversial lyrics, "Eve of Destruction" became the #1 song in America. It was protest at its loudest. "Eve of Destruction" became the anthem of a generation of peace movements and antiwar sit-ins.

The fact that the song was banned in so many places caused Barry to comment a few years later, "I thought that 'Eve of Destruction' was the truth. It was just a bunch of newspaper headlines set to music. It *had* to be sung. It was the first song I'd heard that laid it down just as it was.

"When the song was banned, it showed me that people don't want to know the truth. Isn't that incredible? People want to live in that make-believe dream world, or that Hollywood Playboy fantasy. Happiness is a new home. Happiness is a Ferrari. Happiness is a black book full of phone numbers of pretty girls.

"And when you get down to the nitty gritty, nobody wants to

hear that the human race is about to blow itself from here to Eternity.''

Barry the cynic became even more disillusioned when no one would look at the truth. But the ultimate Truth came to Barry on the street one day in 1970. He and a friend were walking down a Hollywood boulevard on their way to a movie. ''A guy came up to me,'' he recalls, ''and told me that Jesus was coming back.

''I just shined him on, you know. In Hollywood, we called them 'Jesus freaks!' They were everywhere out there. I thought, 'Come on, man. Don't hand me any of that Jesus jazz!'

''But then things started happening. Everywhere I went, I kept being confronted with the name of Jesus Christ. I was at a friend's house one day when I saw a copy of *Good News for Modern Man*. It was a modern translation of the New Testament, but I didn't know that until I had taken it home to read it. I was 35 years old and I had never read a New Testament in my life.

''It blew me away! I discovered the Truth I'd been looking for for so many years. It was Jesus!''

At a party with some old friends one night, ''the ten-thousandth party that week,'' Barry gave up the last hold on his life without Christ.

''I just finally yielded. I asked, 'Jesus, are you really there?'

'' 'Yes.'

'' 'You mean all this time . . .'

'' 'Yes.'

'' 'You mean all these years . . .'

'' 'Yes.'

''Then Christ opened up my memory and showed me all the things that my selfishness had done to other people. All the lives that I'd ruined—people that I'd turned on to drugs.''

Within three weeks, Barry dissolved his contracts with the secular world. He moved out of Hollywood and was soon fellowshiping and studying with a community of Christians in Sanger, California. Barry signed with Myrrh Records to continue his singing career, but this time singing of Jesus Christ as one who knew His power.

Seeds, Barry's first Jesus music album, was released in 1973, eight years after his ''Eve of Destruction.'' Barry began touring with the 2nd Chapter of Acts, and after his second LP, *Lighten Up*, joined the 2nd Chapter for a live album, *To the Bride*. He then moved to Sparrow Records and continued his ministry of Jesus music.

Barry's glowing disposition, his distinctive laugh, and his overall joy became trademarks for a man who was respected throughout the Christian music industry. He told many an audience, "I love being a full moon, reflecting the light of the Son."

11/

"The Rock That Doesn't Roll"

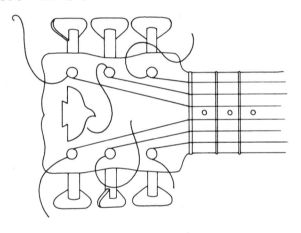

I was lost and blind then a friend of mine
came and took me by the hand
and he led me to his kingdom
that was in another land
now my life has changed it's rearranged
when I think of my past I feel so strange
wowie zowie well He saved my soul
He's the rock that doesn't roll
He's the rock that doesn't roll
well He's good for the body and great for the soul
He's the rock that doesn't roll.

EXPLO '72 WAS, IN A SENSE, THE "COMING OUT" OF CONTEMPORARY Christian music. The fuse had been lit in Dallas. However, there was a long way to go before anything resembling an explosion in Jesus music would take place.

During the next two years or so, Jesus Music was written, recorded and performed, but one would hardly know it by listening to the radio, reading magazines or attending church services. Like a diamond being formed in an underground bed of coal, Jesus music was being purified and molded into a distinct art form under the pressure of a dubious public.

During late 1972 and on through 1974, numerous Christian composers were writing songs and making every possible move to give contemporary Christian music a sound of its own. The writers wanted their music to have the punch of popular music, but they wanted the lyrics to contain more profound substance than the songs of the world.

There were the "radical" composers and performers such as Randy Matthews, Larry Norman, Randy Stonehill, Mike Johnson, and others who desired to write and perform "street music"—rock music with Christians lyrics, a style which parents had trouble endorsing. There were also the artists such as the Archers and Dallas Holm, whose music at that time was contemporary, but carried enough overtones of the more traditional gospel to be accepted by a more general audience. Those more "conservative" musicians— still considered radical by some churches—made up a vital bridge between street music and church music.

Benson Publishing of Nashville was one of the early builders of that bridge. The Archers and Dallas Holm recorded for the Impact label, owned by Benson. While Benson's other label, HeartWarming, carried the traditional family gospel acts such as the Rambos, Impact introduced the more progressive artists.

For a brief period of time, Impact also featured recordings by "street level" artists. Larry Norman's *Upon This Rock* was picked up from Capitol Records and finally made its way into some Christian bookstores (fifth row back, in the corner, behind the greeting cards and next to the water fountain). Graham Kendrick and Judy MacKenzie were folk performers from England whose recordings were picked up and released by Impact Records in

America in 1972. Joshua was the name of a Jesus rock group from the Southwest who recorded one Impact album in 1974 before they disbanded. Impact also featured the music of the Imperials, whose style was basically southern gospel; however, as time went by, the Imperials progressed into a more contemporary mode.

The more conservative musicians performed in numerous churches and crusades around the country, as their music found favor with church leaders. But the radical writers and performers had a much tougher go at it. Their desire to create no-holds-barred Jesus rock met with disdain and oftentimes outright animosity from church elders and the older members of their congregations. Even when those leaders were sympathetic to Jesus music, they were still cautious.

Musician Tom Coomes recalls a 1974 concert in the Blue Church of Philadelphia where caution was the rule. "I was in the group Wing and a Prayer at that time," he recounts. "When we got to the church, we found out that they had never even had drums in that church. Here it was 1974, and we thought the question of drums had long ago been answered. But not at the Blue Church.

"We were asked to meet with the Board of Elders prior to the night's concert. Three of us went in—Tom Stipe, John Mehler and myself. Tom remembers being nervous, but I would say I was somewhat at peace about it. It wasn't like the elders were mad, or that they hated rock music. But they *did* tell us they were very *concerned* that the music we were going to play didn't appeal to the flesh rather than the spirit. They said, 'We've heard about Jesus rock music, and we'll be watching closely.'

"Though the warning was given as a sincere expression of their concern, it had a sound of finality to it! We could have all gotten uptight about the situation, but we didn't. The Lord gave us all a peace at that moment. In fact, I really felt it was a real privilege to be playing there. Our next thought was, should we change our repertoire? We were kind of a rock 'n' roll band. We went off and really prayed. What should we do? Should we do just a worship set? Or a set of mellow music? Or what? We prayed and we really felt a peace about doing just what we usually did.

"That night about 400 or 500 kids crammed into the room," Coomes recalls. "They'd never had that many young people in their church before, ever. We played just what we normally played, which included some rock 'n' roll. But we played it at 1½ on our amps! John, the drummer, did his drum solo, too, but he barely tapped the drums! We could see the elders standing back in the hall. By the second or third number, we could see them smiling!

"About 50 or 60 kids came to know the Lord. As a result, the elders asked us to share with all the adults at the church service that night. Once a month to this day, years afterwards, that church in Philadelphia still has a concert."

The Jesus music writers and performers knew what they had to do, regardless of the consequences. They had to write the songs that the Lord had given them to write; they had to perform the music that would reach the churched *and* unchurched youth; and they had to upgrade the quality of a fledgling art form.

Bob Hartman was a member of Petra, one of the first all-out Jesus rock bands to record an album. He described Petra's reasons for existence. "We're extremely rock-oriented, but we're not oppressively heavy. The name 'Petra' has a deeper meaning to us because it's a word that's used in the Bible when Jesus said, 'Upon this rock I will build my church.' That word 'rock' is 'petra' in Greek. It's upon the confession of Jesus Christ being Lord of a person's life that our group is built, because of the experience that we have had with Him. He's changed our lives and given us a whole new outlook on life, and that outlook is reflected in our music."

Petra's music was rock, all right, but with its special spiritual dimensions it became a way of life for young rock music fans.

"People," Bob continued, "have almost been brainwashed by other rock groups and the message they have to bring. I think it's time the people heard a positive message."

A yet harder rock group was Agape, whose two albums were released in 1971 and 1972 during the crest of the Jesus Movement. They played Jesus rock at its crustiest—music which cut through the thickest defenses of the non-Christian rock fans. For those to whom hard rock music was a language, Agape and Petra spoke—clearly. As a result, many young people, whose main defense against Christianity was its "old fashioned, hokey" music, found themselves pleasantly surprised when a friend shared Jesus rock music with them.

Agape's and Petra's music was not the most welcomed form of music on Christian radio stations, either. Only a few such stations would even consider playing their songs. One of those few stations was KDTX-FM in Dallas.

KDTX had broadcast all of the Cotton Bowl meetings of Explo '72. Station manager Mike Burk was impressed by the contemporary gospel music he heard play there, and the way the youth responded to it. Mike opened up the 10 p.m. to 2 a.m. air shift for a Jesus music show, and invited me to host it. On a fall night in 1972, "A Joyful Noise" became a live, four-hour nightly radio show in Dallas.

I opened the first show with a song by Myrrh recording group First Gear, appropriately entitled "Ain't No Stoppin' Us Now." For the first few nights, there were a few calls of complaint about the rock music, but the calls of encouragement and thanks quickly overshadowed them. Dallas had been primed by Explo, and Jesus music filled the air nightly.

"A Joyful Noise" in Dallas became much more than just a music show. Top Christian performers were interviewed, including Andraé Crouch, Noel Paul Stookey, rock artist Chi Coltrane, and many more. Since KDTX had large studios, numerous live concerts were also broadcast as part of "A Joyful Noise." Larry Norman, Paul Clark, Ken Medema, Malcolm & Alwyn, and countless other Jesus music artists performed. Sometimes the concerts were announced far in advance, and large crowds attended. Other times, spontaneous concerts were arranged when a musician passed through, and a handful of people showed up in time. But all the concerts were heard by thousands of radio listeners in north Texas over KDTX.

Much as "The Scott Ross Show" had done in New York state, "A Joyful Noise" provided nightly fellowship for young people and adults who preferred Christian radio over secular radio. "A Joyful Noise" continued on the air live for one year in Dallas, but KDTX (later KMGC) would broadcast nightly Jesus music for a while longer.

Meanwhile, in Washington, an innovation was being tried. In May of 1973, WCTN introduced a format of secular adult rock and contemporary Christian music combined. However, Christians in the Washington area proved to be extremely conservative. The unique format lasted only a few months, before WCTN had to change to a more moderate playlist as the CBN stations in New

York had been forced to do a few years earlier. The Jesus music stayed, but in smaller amounts.

Still, whenever Jesus music was broadcast, there were changed lives. Sometimes it only took a few moments of exposure to lead someone to the startling realization that Jesus was the answer.

Friends:

I was driving from Oklahoma City to Clinton, Oklahoma, one day after being on a hard drug trip for the whole weekend, when I turned on the radio to KOMA. It was 6:30 in the morning, and I was expecting to find my usual heavy rock—but as I listened closer to the words of this different kind of rock and roll, I heard a different kind of message. A message about a person called Jesus. I started to change the station as I have for the last 25 years. But instead, this time I listened.

After hearing such a *beautiful* message from people like myself, I started to realize that Jesus is a more real thing than reality itself.

My life has changed a lot now, as I have thrown away my man-made drugs and taken on God's love instead.

Well, I'm sure you know the rest of the story . . . How can I say thank you but to say that *I love you all very much.* You people are beautiful and the message you carry is so super concrete.

J.W., Medicine Park, Oklahoma

In spite of the testimonies of young people who found Christ through Jesus music, the battle against it went on. Certain evangelists would incite young people to literally burn anything resembling or alluding to rock music. There even were bonfires held for the occasion.

Evangelist Bob Larson was probably the most outspoken critic of rock music in the late 1960s and 1970s. Larson, himself a musician, wrote a book as early as 1967 denouncing rock and roll music as "the devil's diversion." His scathing criticisms of rock music rapidly resulted in support from the adult/parent side, while many teenagers scorned Larson.

Rock & Roll: The Devil's Diversion was followed by several more books on the evils of rock and roll: *Rock & The Church* (1971), *Hippies, Hindus and Rock & Roll* (1970) and *The Day the*

Music Died (1973). Larson lectured at churches and high schools, playing demonstrations of rock music, speaking against it and encouraging young people to destroy their rock records by burning them.

Larson's fiery antirock campaign was highly publicized by both the secular and religious press. The secular press was skeptical or critical; the religious press was generally sympathetic. However, Larson was anything but sympathetic toward Christian rock. In his book *Rock & The Church,* Larson laid down this indictment: "I maintain that the use of Christian rock is a blatant compromise so obvious that only those who are spiritually blind by carnality can accept it."[1]

He added:

The phenomenon of Christian rock has been around only since approximately 1968. There is still some question whether or not decisions in Christian rock concerts lead to genuine rebirth. Usually there is no clear-cut invitation to repentance at such affairs. If the explanation of steps of salvation is blurred, how can the way be found?

Some have speculated that more often than not, conversion to Christ at Christian rock concerts and musicals is not really a born-again experience but an identification with the person of Jesus within the perspective of the "groovy Christian life." [2]

Although many of Larson's arguments against *secular* rock were well-founded, he created great resentment among *Christian* rock musicians with blanketing conclusions such as: "Once the possibility of demon involvement is suggested, there is no way Christian rock can be justified." [3]

Other evangelists joined in denouncing rock, and the gap widened. The main support for the antirock preachers came from adults and parents who disliked rock and roll in the first place, and the antirock music books and lectures gave them what they believed to be a biblical foundation for the abhorrence of all rock music, including Jesus music.

The Jesus musicians who witnessed and had a part in the conversion of young people through their music were not as ready to criticize the more avant garde styles of rock gospel. Even though they themselves may not have favored all of its forms, they saw the fruits of such evangelism.

Chuck Girard, with a background in rock music, commented in 1973, "I believe God may call some hard rock band, and I believe they may do all hard rock 'n' roll, screaming Jesus lyrics. That may be all they do. I believe that where they'll be used is a different place than where we'll be used.

"I think it would be very hard for me," he continued, "if I were 55 or 62, to believe right off the bat that this is all right on. Because I think some of it isn't. But I think it's hard for some of the older people to grasp the sincerity of the long-haired Christians at first, especially in light of the counterculture movement out of which grew the tradition of long hair and hard rock music.

"I've had a lot of old people come up and say, 'Well, if Jesus has changed you on the inside, why doesn't he change you on the outside?' They should realize that God looks on the inner man.

"I think as everything progresses and they see that there are long-haired Christians sticking with it, faithful to the Lord, and being used as ministers, they'll understand it more."

Cornerstone, a paper published by the Jesus People USA, printed this letter to the editors:

> Until this past year, both of us thought being a Christian was pretty bad, no good music, old hymnbooks and a Bible that was written in old English. Not very much to interest people who were into living in the present. It wasn't until after I met Jesus and was born again that we met some other Christians who shared Larry Norman, *Cornerstone* and the Holy Spirit. So Christianity wasn't dead after all! Unsaved people hardly ever hear about this side—the true life of joy of living for Jesus in today's world, not 400 years ago.
>
> D. & C. H.
> Sarasota, Florida[4]

Cornerstone was one of the "underground" Jesus papers which published the Good News in a most unique way. The paper was sponsored by the Jesus People USA in Chicago, who also formed The Resurrection Band. The band, which specialized in hard rock Christian message music, began their ministry in 1971, playing in high schools, prisons, and in the streets.

The Resurrection Band, *Cornerstone,* and JPUSA's drama troupe, "The Holy Ghost Players," were the most adventurous when it came to boldness in communicating the gospel. From the mod-art design of their newspaper to the screaming guitars in their band, they dealt in forms of communication which were controversial to say the least.

Contrary to the bad images of Christian rock 'n' rollers given by the antirock evangelists, these same young people were consistently more outspoken and bold in their presentation of the life-saving claims of Jesus than most Christians. The complaints against the raucousness of their music and the admonition that no one could use rock music to witness to the unsaved became mighty weak when the work of JPUSA was studied deeply, with literally thousands of people won to Christ through their ministry.

As the heated controversy continued, undaunted young composers kept at their work, creating what they were convinced the Lord wanted them to create. Because of the lack of support, there was little money in their work, and it was next to impossible to make more than a meager living as a professional contemporary Christian musician. This kept Jesus music a fairly pure art form, practically devoid of the corruption which existed in so many other forms of music, including some religious music.

Though Jesus music had been shunned by the majority of church leaders, young people were finding out about it, mostly by word-of-mouth. The exposure of the music on the radio still proved to be next to impossible, and the increasing number of Jesus music records were still hard to find in stores.

The proprietors of the secular record stores, however, had every right to refuse much of the Jesus music. Since the music was still in its fledgling stage, many of the albums being released were poor in quality. The spirit of the singers was not enough to qualify the albums as professional recordings, especially when the technical and musical quality of those albums was poor.

Also, many times the youth, in their crusade for Jesus music, became overexuberant and presumptuously expected their churches to accept the new kind of music too readily and without question. Unfortunately, there were not many adults who understood contemporary music enough to give them unbiased guidance which would encourage the young people in their musical pursuits, but at the same time calm their youthful overzealousness. In that sense, the young Christians had to make a go of it on their own.

12/

"All Day Dinner"

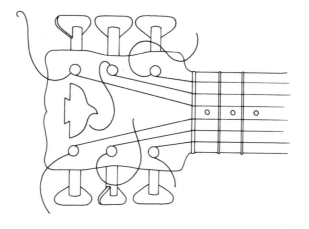

We might sing it country for a thousand years
Then progress to opera for the cultured ones there
The King perhaps will then conduct the jubilee band
Then we'll march around the city of this musical land
We'll all sing a new song
Lord, what a morning can't wait to hear that melody
He's written a new scale
Do-re-me-fa-so-la-te-do-no!
Can't you hear that heavenly harmony
We'll sing ten octaves lower than any bass singer's
dream
The music will rise, soar to the sky, unlimited highs
At that eternal gospel singin'
All day dinner on the ground.

Dᴜʀɪɴɢ ᴛʜᴇ 1800s ᴀɴᴅ ᴇᴀʀʟʏ 1900s ᴀᴍᴇʀɪᴄᴀɴ Cʜʀɪsᴛɪᴀɴ ꜰᴇʟʟᴏᴡsʜɪᴘ relied heavily upon the church. Before the relatively recent advent of air-conditioned church sanctuaries, congregations would join together outside in the hopefully breezy air to praise the Lord with "all-day singing and dinner on the ground." Church revivals would be held outdoors under the thatched roofs of outdoor worship pavilions. On Church Picnic Weekend, whole families would climb into their buggies, wagons, and automobiles, and head out to the lake or assembly grounds for a day of fun and games, and rib-sticking food.

By the mid-1960s, though, most Sunday church meetings were back in the sanctuaries, at a year-round 72°. The brush arbors were hardly more than memories. A new form of fellowship grew out of the Jesus Movement in the 1970s, however, which got the people back together outdoors to praise the Lord, sing, learn, and generally have a great time. Though the scene was quite different from the camp meetings of the earlier generations, the spirit of fellowship was just as evident in the outdoor "Jesus festivals."

It was natural that the Jesus festivals should grow out of the Jesus Movement in the '70s. Not only did the Movement itself start on the streets, on the "outside"; it also grew out of a generation enamored by the giant secular Monterey Pop Festival in California and the even more gigantic Woodstock festival of 1969, where reportedly more than 500,000 young people attended.

Festivals such as Woodstock were mass outdoor gatherings where young people retreated to their own world—a world virtually void of any reminder of the Establishment, except for the policemen and the chagrined residents of nearby communities. The festivals were meccas for youth who were seeking new solutions in their quest for love, peace, and often total escape from the world.

Monterey and Woodstock led to other secular festivals: the Palm Beach Rock Festival in 1969; the Atlanta International Pop Festival in 1970 (attended by 200,000), the Pocono Rock Festival in 1972, and numerous others.

However, at an Altamont, California, rockfest in 1969, the utopian dream of peace, love, and brotherhood began to decay. A man was murdered by Hell's Angels directly in front of the stage where the Rolling Stones were playing before the giant crowd. The band played on, but the rock festivals were somehow never again the same. Festival promoters had more and more trouble finding places to have them, and ultimately learned to move the concerts each year to avoid confronting the same constables. Gigantic crowds of people continued to attend the rock festivals, but the events often became no more than havens for drug abuse, or at best havens of rock music.

Except for the finale concert of Explo '72 in Dallas, Jesus festivals never reached the gigantic proportions of the rock festivals. But the organizers did experience a greater degree of support from landowners and host communities. The Jesus festival crowds proved to be cleaner, more polite, more sober, and less rowdy. The members of the Establishment were the lawmakers. Their sympathies tended to favor youth whose beliefs were somewhat within the limits of what even the elders were familiar with—the Christian faith. The new music was different than the earlier generations', but tolerable because of the familiar message.

The first major Jesus festival was the Faith Festival in Evansville, Indiana, in March of 1970. More than 6,000 people were present in a stadium to hear Pat Boone and his family, Christian folk singer Gene Cotton, Jesus rock artists Danny Taylor, Larry Norman, Crimson Bridge, and "e." In 1971, the event was repeated and 15,000 people attended. The 1971 Faith Festival was covered by CBS television.

Later, in May, the Love Song Festival at Knott's Berry Farm drew 20,000 people to a Southern California amusement park, marking Knott's largest nighttime attendance in its 53-year history. Several Jesus music groups out of Calvary Chapel performed that historic night in various parts of the park. They included Love Song, The Way, Blessed Hope and Children of the Day.

The Knott's Love Song Festival began a California tradition of amusement park Jesus festivals. Special tickets were sold for use on all the park rides and Christian folk and rock music wafted through the park from various strategically located performing stages. The success of their first event prompted the proprietors of Knott's Berry Farm to stage the Christian music nights more often. At first, they were Love Song Festivals, but then became known as Maranatha Night at Knott's, due to the use of musical groups from Calvary Chapel's Maranatha! Music Ministry. For the next three years, three festival nights were staged annually—one in the spring, one in the fall, and one on New Year's Eve.

Californians were accustomed to the fun and flash of entertainment, and the Maranatha Music Nights provided an excellent form of Christian entertainment. There were no Bible teachings or baptisms at the amusement park festivals, nor was there much congregational worship. The southern California youth had those forms of fellowship and worship waiting for them back at their home churches, especially Calvary Chapel.

But for young people in other parts of the country, there were often no churches such as Calvary Chapel—churches which opened their doors to barefooted, blue-jeaned teens who needed acceptance. The festivals *became* church for many young people—outdoor sanctuaries with the sky as a canopy. For many people, the Jesus festivals marked the beginning of new lives in Christ.

In August of 1973, a central Pennsylvania potato field became one of those sanctuaries. Mennonite Harold Zimmerman organized Jesus '73, the start of an annual tradition. Jesus '73 featured three days of festival, with guest appearances by top name Christian musicians and speakers.

Young people and some adults of all faiths attended Jesus '73. The breaking down of denominational barriers had already become a trait of the Jesus people. Baptists worshiped with Assembly of God members; Catholics fellowshiped with Mennonites. Musicians from the Church of the Nazarene played before Presbyterians; gospel performers from the Church of God in Christ sang for Methodists. In the midst of them all, there was a large number of non-Christians who heard the gospel and responded to it.

Jesus '73 spanned three days. Through makeshift entrance gates set up in a field passed festival-goers in automobiles, trucks, vans, Winnebagos, on motorcycles, and even on horseback. There were numerous hitch-hikers, too. From all over America and from overseas people came to join in the fellowship. Visitors stopped at the entrance gates, registered, and received their "welcome packets" with information on who would be singing when, where to go for first aid, and what *not* to do while visiting the festival. By the time the first music group struck up a chord on the giant stage, a tent city stood where there used to be farmland. Rows and rows of campers, tents, and cars fashioned a pattern of lines which stretched over the next hill. A blue haze filled the air as campfires flickered throughout the campsites.

After the tents had been pitched, everyone filed to the concert area to hear and see the Christian singing groups and solo artists perform and ministers speak. For the next few days, the people present at the festival would be in a world completely different than the one from which they came. Musicians performing at Jesus '73 included Andraé Crouch and the Disciples, Danny Lee and the Children of Truth, Danny Taylor, Randy Matthews, Randy Stonehill, and others—many of the same performers who had appeared at Explo '72.

Jerry Bryant, who later became host of the nationally syndicated Jesus rock radio show, "Jesus—Solid Rock," sold records at Jesus '73. "I phoned all the religious record companies I could think of," he recalls, "and told them 'Send me everything you've got.' Of course, I meant contemporary music, and in those days, there wasn't much! Just Larry Norman, Love Song, and a few others.

"So, I loaded up a Winnebago we had rented for the occasion, and carted all the albums to Jesus '73. We were packed to the gills with records, so much that the camper leaned to one side. We set up our record display, with the traditional gospel on one side and the Jesus music on the other.

"People freaked out. 'Where did you get all this stuff? We've never heard of it!' By the end of the first day, all of the contemporary records were sold."

An estimated 8,000 people attended Jesus '73. The music they heard, in many cases for the first time, was contemporary Christian music. As each person returned home, the news of Jesus music spread. One year later, Jesus '74 drew twice as many people to Pennsylvania as its '73 predecessor.

Twenty-five hundred miles away, at the Orange County Fairgrounds in Costa Mesa, California, Praise '74 attracted an estimated 16,000 people. Praise '74 was a combination Jesus festival/fair, with daily outdoor stadium concerts, Christian arts and crafts exhibits, and a steady program of quality Christian films.

John Styll, whose radio show "Hour of Praise" on KGER was the pioneer Jesus music show in southern California, recalled that Praise '74 helped to introduce varied California talent, rather than solely Maranatha groups as had the amusement park festivals.

"Praise '74 was sponsored by Maranatha Village," he adds, "a local Christian bookstore which grew out of the Jesus Movement. The festival featured Andraé Crouch and the Disciples, Terry Talbot and the Branch Bible Band, Love Song, the Latinos, Ralph Carmichael, Cam Floria, Jerry Sinclair, and numerous other musicians.'' Disneyland fireworks a few miles off lit up the sky behind the stage each night while explosive Jesus music filled the stadium.

In the summer of 1975, Cam Floria and Bill Rayborn designed and sponsored the First Annual Christian Artists' Seminar in the Rockies, held at a YMCA camp in the mountain resort town of Estes Park, Colorado. There was an abundance of music and talent: the gathering featured Evie Tornquist, Andraé Crouch and the Disciples, the Archers, the Continental Singers, Jeremiah People, the Imperials, the Hawaiians, and a wide array of other performers.

The Seminar was unlike any of its Jesus festival progenitors, however, in that it catered more heavily to the musicians and other members of organized churches and colleges and their music than to the Christian ''street people'' whose tastes leaned to Jesus music. Also, the Seminar was not intended to be a festival to draw in music *fans,* except for the evening concerts. Rather, the Seminar was mainly intended for people in music ministries.

In the ensuing years, the Seminar, referred to around the country simply as ''Estes Park,'' would increase greatly from the 1975 attendance of approximately 800. Seminar leaders trained musicians, music ministers, and choir directors. Concerts at night featured a potpourri of artists running the gamut from classical to rock, and a ''National Talent Competition'' was begun, with cash prizes and recording contracts going to the victors. Probably the most important contribution the annual gathering offered was a much-needed time of fellowship between musicians. For some, it was the only true retreat for fellowship they had during the year.

1975 was also the year that Jesus festivals sprang up everywhere. There was Jesus '75 in Pennsylvania, where rain turned the festival grounds into a quagmire of mud, though it failed to dampen the festival-goers' spirits. In Michigan, Salt '75 featured ''25 hours of music, teaching, Bible study and prayer.'' The music was performed by Simple Truth, Randy Matthews, Good News Circle, Oreon, Honeytree, the Continental Singers, and others.

At the northern end of the Blue Ridge Parkway, Fishnet '75 began what was to be a yearly pilgrimage for many Americans to

Front Royal, Virginia. Elsewhere that year, Jesus '75 Midwest was held in St. Louis, the Sonshine Festival in Ohio, Lodestone in Vancouver, B.C., and the Road Home Celebration in Colorado Springs, in the shadow of Pikes Peak.

In California, the Maranatha Nights continued at Knott's Berry Farm. At the Joyland Amusement Park in Wichita, Kansas, the first Jesus Festival of Joy drew around 3,000 people. In Texas, the Hill Country Faith Festival featured Terry Talbot, Liberation Suite, Jamie Owens, and Children of Faith.

As each year passed, more and more ambitious promoters and would-be promoters attempted to program festivals of Jesus music. Some succeeded, some failed. The events were held in stadiums, mountain glens, orange groves, amusement parks, fairgrounds, racetracks, rodeo arenas, campuses, and beaches. Most of them featured musicians and ministers offering praise, worship and learning experiences. Communions, baptisms, and altar calls were often included. Communion grape juice was served in specially packaged creamer cups by a dairy for a Florida festival, and baptisms were often held in rivers and farm ponds.

The festivals should have been the envy of thousands of ministers across the country who saw the free interchange between people of so many varied faiths. In some cases, that was the feeling. However, in other instances, church ministers refused any support for fear the youth would be "caught up" in someone else's religion.

The fears of proselytism could not be ignored. Some churches had lost their youth to the Jesus movement, and the Jesus festivals became about the only spiritual nourishment some youth ever got. Over the years, however, many of the skeptical churches began sponsoring busloads of their youth to the festivals, providing adult supervision and guidance. Such church efforts resulted in a melting of many barriers, as the adults were able to explain the differences which existed in the varied faiths and persuasions. The interdenominational fellowship was invaluable for youths in understanding other faiths. People who attended the festivals testified to the life-changing experiences they encountered.

At Jesus '74 I had my first encounter with God's love. Boy, was I surprised! Everywhere I went, there was love shining forth—in our camp, in many long lines, and in problems. "Praise God!" was on the lips and faces of those near me. I just had to know the source of this love and joy. So I asked Jesus to fill my heart and become Lord of my life. He did. Praise the Lord!

Last year at Jesus '75 the Lord's love and power was also manifest in many ways. Even through rain storms, mud and all the resulting difficulties, He showed His love and power. In love He taught us to look only to Him, put our trust in Him and to praise and thank Him in *all* circumstances. It really works! He used the mud in a very special way, to help my mother to come to see and know His love and to become her Lord.[1]

Memories such as this one helped one forget the sunburns, the poison ivy rashes, the cut feet, the bugs, and sometimes rain and mud to boot. The adversities were of little import when one was being saturated with Christian love, fine music, Bible teaching, new friendships, great fellowship, and often, changed lives.

13/

"Let Us Be One"

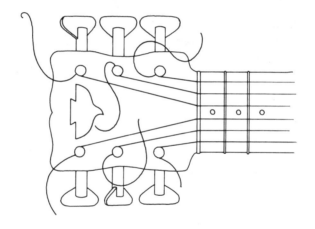

Lord, don't let me strive against my brother
I'm so tired of it, don't want to do it no more
Lord, don't let us fight against each other
Let us be one in you
Lord, give us love for one another
In what we say, yes, and what we do
Lord, teach us to build up one another
Let us be one in you
For your sake, let us learn to wait
On the Spirit's move
We know that the hour is so late
And you'll be comin' soon
Lord, let us rest up in your Spirit
Knowing full well that we're in your hands
Oh God, open up our hearts so we can hear it
Let us be one in you

KYMS. "THE ORANGE 106." IT WAS A SMALL FM STATION LOCATED in Santa Ana, California. The music was "underground" rock, and the owners were having problems competing with 77 other radio stations in the Los Angeles/Orange County area.

KYMS was one of four stations owned by Southwestern Broadcasters, Inc. The president of Southwestern was on the verge of giving up in the battle to win enough of a loyal audience to show up in the ratings books. About that time, someone suggested that KYMS could become a religious station.

Orange County was reported to have one of the highest ratios of Christians in the nation. It would seem that a contemporary religious station concept would have become reality for that area much sooner, but there had been none, except for one or two Jesus music radio shows. Since May 10, 1974, John Styll had broadcast "Hour of Praise" on KGER in Long Beach, a traditional religious station which carried back-to-back preaching programs, much like most other religious stations in the country. John's show was on each afternoon at 3:00 p.m. He would go into his studio in Newport Beach at ProMedia Productions, usually after lunch, and record the hour show on a ten-inch reel of tape. Then, the rush was on.

The scene was somewhat reminiscent of an old Tom Mix cowboy movie, when the star literally jumped onto his horse and rode off to save the train. Except, in this case, John ran out into the parking lot with his 10″ reel of tape; literally jumped *into* his Mustang and drove through the traffic-filled streets from Newport Beach to KGER's Long Beach studios via the most direct route possible.

More than once, John and the tape arrived as the closing comments were being made on the taped show leading up to "Hour of Praise." The on-air announcer had long before learned to have an album of contemporary music queued up in case John didn't make it. But, as he is proud to admit, he always made it!

"Hour of Praise ran on KGER for exactly one year," John explains. "It was both a vanguard show and an avant-garde show."

Just before "Hour of Praise" ended its year run on KGER, speculation began about what was happening at KYMS in Santa Ana. Finally, the news was announced: KYMS was going to change from secular rock music to contemporary Christian music—one of the first stations in America to do so.

On March 15, 1975, KYMS, the "Orange 106," became the "Spirit of 106." Arnie McClatchey, station manager for KYMS, recalls the public's reaction. "The sound on the air excited the young, Christian populace of Orange County," he remembers. "KYMS quickly became *their* station, freely playing the Jesus music which had been impossible to hear on radio before, except for an hour or so each day."

Some of Calvary Chapel's concerts were broadcast live on KYMS, almost immediately drawing the attention of the young people. Also, a remote radio studio was built at Maranatha Village, the Christian shopping center located in the original Calvary Chapel building, which had been sold to businessman Jim Willems when the Calvary crowds outgrew the facilities.

Only nine days before KYMS' debut as a contemporary Christian radio station, Larry King and several associates had introduced KBHL-FM, "The Sound of the New Life," to Lincoln, Nebraska.

KBHL went on the air at 6:00 p.m. on March 6, 1975. "We're on the air! Thank You, Lord!" Those were the first words heard at 95.3 FM. In the next few weeks, the station was deluged with calls of approval from all over the Lincoln listening area. Local businesses, including the A&W restaurant, distributed KBHL bumper stickers, which stated that KBHL was "*Kept By His Love*." Automobile bumpers all over Lincoln spread the news of KBHL's arrival on the scene. Brilliant orange T-shirts emblazoned with KBHL's call letters and a frosty mug of A&W root beer told the people that both were "Thirst Quenchers." It wasn't long until the station began sponsoring contemporary Christian concerts by 2nd Chapter of Acts, Barry McGuire, and numerous other well-known artists.

KBHL's activities in promoting the new Christian music marked a major step forward, as did those of KYMS. Enlisting top-name business establishments for major promotions of Christian radio stations had been done before, but never for Jesus music.

Contemporary radio was a medium very much akin to Jesus music. Like Jesus musicians, the main goal and desire of these contemporary broadcasters was to enable everyone to make their faith a part of their daily life. They wanted to present radio as part of a Christian life style, one which was not ostentatious. The new Christian life style would allow teenagers an opportunity to witness to their friends without being excessively verbal. Their music witnessed, but was not a turn-off, because it so closely paralleled pop music in style. A person could keep his radio on the contemporary Christian station without being ashamed of it in front of his peers.

The apostle Paul stated, "I am not ashamed of the gospel, for it is the power of God for salvation to everyone who believes . . ." (Rom. 1:16, NAS). Likewise, the young people of the 1970s were not ashamed of the gospel, but they were embarrassed when they had to couch it in what to them was an antiquated music style or broadcasting style. For the youth, life in Christ was as exciting and real in the 1970s as ever before, and they needed to convey that as well as live it.

So, the solution to them was to take the venerable gospel message and run it as a thread through the fabric of their lives. Contemporary music and contemporary radio provided the necessary atmosphere. Listeners could tune into KBHL, KYMS, or one of several other new contemporary Christian stations and "participate" in radio as they did with the secular stations. News, weather, sports, music, personalities and even contests provided the Christians with a companion—a Christian alternative.

The new contemporary stations usually didn't limit their programming to Jesus rock music alone. In fact, a fairly strict hand was kept on how "far out" the music was. Moderation was the rule. To balance the music and the audience, the station programmers generally played music which could best be described as MOR (middle-of-the-road). In one deejay's words, it had to be "not too rocky and not too hokey."

The result of this MOR approach was best described in a letter to the editor of the *Lincoln Star*. In part, it read:

> Anyone who is a Christian and hasn't yet discovered KBHL has been missing a very delightful and spiritual experience for over a month. If one is not yet a Christian, he should find out what this "new life" sounds like. There is nothing to lose, and everything to gain.
>
> Those within the age group of one to 100 will find themselves participating happily in the worship of our Lord and Savior, Jesus Christ. The youth begin to listen to those old favorites that have been passed down through the years, with new regard and appreciation. The not-so-young among us soon begin hearing with a new attitude those newer contemporary hymns of praise to God.[1]

Houston, Texas, was another city to be served by a contemporary Christian station in 1975. Benton White, who along with Scott Campbell, Rod Hunter and Dewey Boynton helped to create the new contemporary format, experienced varied reactions of KFMK listeners.

"When the Houston station went on the air with the new format," recalls Benton, "there was nothing else like it there. The company, Crawford Broadcasting, wanted something new and exciting. They wanted to pioneer. So, when the opportunity came, they took it.

"KFMK went totally music from 6 a.m. to midnight, with mainly contemporary Christian music. Because of our lack of enough Jesus music records in our station library, we really were fairly moderate to start with, kind of middle-of-the-road music.

"Being at the age I was, which was 22, I was looking for something which spoke to a young age group. To see the possibilities of the Word of Christ being spread in that way, was something I wanted to be a part of from the ground up."

Jesus music activity was on the increase. Residents of Santa Ana, Lincoln, Houston, and a few other cities could now experience contemporary music more than ever. One major problem still existed, however. People at one end of the country still didn't know what was happening at the other end. Things had been that way since the beginning of Jesus music.

Singer Danny Taylor, whose early years in Jesus music were spent in the Northeast, recalls how little he knew of the activities in the western U. S. "In 1969, we really had no models," Danny says. "For example, there was Scott Ross, myself, Larry Black, Charles McPheeters, and Mike Johnson. Mike was with the Exkursions out of Pittsburgh. The Exkursions were just about the earliest group out of the eastern U. S. to perform Jesus music. Anyway, all of our paths would cross doing different things.

"We weren't really aware of what was going on, until the Faith Festival at Evansville, Indiana, in 1970, when I did the concert there with Larry Norman, Bob MacKenzie, Thurlow Spurr, Crimson Bridge, and a group which was very heavy for the time, called 'e.'

"We had the feeling on the East Coast that we were primarily doing the whole thing as far as radio was concerned. 'The Scott

Ross Show' was becoming a model for the East Coast at least. But, in reality, things happened slowly. The East Coast had traditionally been quite conservative, and it was a lot harder to break through there. It was in 1971, when we became aware of Love Song, that we became more aware of what was happening elsewhere. We started hearing stories of Costa Mesa, the Church on the Way, and other places.''

Meanwhile, Californian Tom Stipe was working as a young minister at Calvary Chapel in Costa Mesa. "In the early days," he remembers, "there was such a personal, central movement in Southern California, in terms of incredible spiritual activity, there was little awareness of what was going on everywhere else. There was such a rush of media attention, every time we'd turn around the TV cameras would be set up at church, telecasting pictures of all the kids raising their hands in praise. It was an oddity for the press.

"As soon as a Jesus music group got together, they would begin thinking 'Well, this is nice but I wonder if we could go play someplace outside of California.' Then they started realizing some of the things that were going on elsewhere in the country.

"As the groups got together and we felt like we were being used sufficiently in southern California, we began to turn our attentions outward. This came in about 1972, when Love Song did their first national tour in 1972 with Ray Johnson. Ray booked the tour from Houston, and everybody was amazed! They went as far as Texas!

"Love Song would come back from their tours and tell all of us in California what was happening in the rest of the country. I remember the guys coming back describing how contemporary music was being played on the radio. They told us about Scott Ross, and spoke of his earlier days at Shea Stadium emceeing the Beatles concert. That was our first impression that someone in the professional world was stepping in and taking a stand for the Lord and utilizing his talents to the glory of God.

"Later, there was considerable interest from Atlantic Records in New York City. Ahmet Ertegun, the president of Atlantic at that time and producer of top groups like Crosby, Stills and Nash, offered Love Song an incredible deal to be on Atlantic Records. It was the same time the group members were in final negotiations with Good News Records in California. At this point, we realized that all this was going to spread out. We realized it *was* spreading out!''

Meanwhile, Phil Keaggy, who had played guitar and sung with a Cleveland rock group, Glass Harp, recorded his first solo album in 1973 as the debut recording on New Song records. It was titled *What a Day*. New Song Records was an outreach ministry of the Love Inn community in Freeville, where the Scott Ross Show originated.

"When guitarist Phil Keaggy had his short stint with Love Song around 1973," Tom Stipe recalls, "I remember the incredible excitement of having Phil walk in the door from a completely different part of the country, and it blew us all away at Calvary Chapel. Pastor Chuck Smith still remembers the Monday night that Phil played."

Many people agreed that the Lord was busy with both the East Coast and the West Coast, and the main tie between them was the musicians and their relationships. To improve national intercommunication, twenty men from across the country and from various branches of Christian work met in Fort Wayne, Indiana, in April of 1975 to discuss a change. Paul Craig Paino, Jr., a minister at Calvary Temple in Fort Wayne, called the meeting, which resulted in the formation of the Fellowship of Contemporary Christian Ministries (FCCM). According to Paul, "The FCCM was born out of a desire to see the segmented ministries of the contemporary outreaches brought together under a common mode of communication and fellowship."

The organization of FCCM was a milestone in Jesus music history, for the communication between the east coast and the west coast would improve, it was hoped. Also, beginning in 1976, the FCCM would sponsor annual summer conferences. These three-day retreats allowed musicians, concert promoters, coffeehouse ministers, theater groups, record company representatives, broadcasters, artists' managers, recording studio engineers, and anyone else who took contemporary Christian ministries seriously, to participate in a yearly fellowship with the brothers and sisters in common ministries throughout America.

An official newsletter was circulated among new members as a form of network, designed to facilitate communication between ministries. The newsletter was more or less a collection of epistles between members, sharing failures as well as successes.

Lou Hancherick, one of the twenty charter members of the

FCCM who attended the Fort Wayne meeting in 1975, had a vision to keep not only FCCM members informed as to what was happening in the world of Jesus music, but to keep the general public informed as well. Lou announced his intentions to publish a magazine titled *Harmony*.

There had been a Jesus Music magazine before. In 1971, *Rock In Jesus* had been created. A total of five issues of *RIJ* were published, but the readership was much less than *Harmony* would later enjoy. *Rock In Jesus* was married with *Right On!* in January of 1973, and continued for a while as a middle section of the Berkeley paper.

Except for *Rock In Jesus*, Jesus music had received very limited specialized coverage in secular or Christian publications. Most of the Christian press which ran any articles ran antirock and anti-Jesus music stories. The stories were written for the traditional clientele of those publications—people who were already against rock music.

There were a few exceptions. Cheryl Forbes in *Christianity Today* gave critical but generally positive reviews of Jesus music album releases. Occasionally, *Campus Life* magazine, the top Christian teen magazine, would feature an article about or by Jesus music artists, but to no regular degree.

So, in May of 1975, the first issue of *Harmony* was a sight for sore eyes—a cause for celebration among Jesus musicians and contemporary Christians. Now fans had an opportunity to read a magazine from cover to cover, and keep on top of everything happening in Jesus music.

Dan Hickling, the editor of *Harmony*'s first issue, had worked with publisher Lou Hancherick since August of 1974 in preparing the magazine. Dan edited *Harmony* during a layoff from the Buffalo Ford Motor Company plant. The layoff was very timely for the *Harmony* project, but it meant tight times for the Hicklings.

"It was almost a full-time job," Dan related, "just trying to find out what was happening in Jesus music. Until 1975, we had hardly any communication from the record companies. I wanted *Harmony* to be a forum for information and exchange of ideas between artists and others involved in contemporary Christian ministries. My position was in the ministry of helps, especially helping people to establish contact with other people it was necessary for them to know."

Harmony's first issue appropriately featured Randy Matthews, one of Jesus music's pioneers, on the cover. Inside were an interview with Bob Hartman of Petra, a "Tuning Up" column authored by Danny Taylor, reviews of six new Jesus music albums, assorted news releases, and the first part of "Brand New Song," the history of Jesus music by one Paul Baker.

Harmony, KYMS, KBHL, KFMK, and the FCCM all contributed in making 1975 a milestone year for Jesus music. The year marked the beginning of a stupendous growth period for *all* forms of gospel music. But the most dramatic increase would be noted in *contemporary* Christian music.

14/

"Super Star"

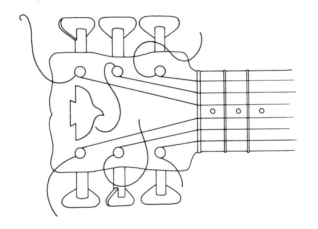

I don't wanna' be a super star
All I want to do is shine
With the light of Jesus
Walking in a path that's mine
There's a special place for me
And in the spotlight it may well be
But if no one ever hears my name
I'll be shinin' just the same.
I don't wanna' reach for mountain tops
If Jesus isn't there with me
But I'll reach higher than the sky
If that's where I'm supposed to be
I'm not lookin' for a big applause
If it's gonna' be a super star
Then let it be for Him, for Him.

SUPER STAR
Words and Music by Scott Wesley Brown, Randy Matthews, and Michael C. Johnson. © Copyright 1976 by LifeSong
Music Press and Paragon Music Corp. New Bay Psalter Music Press. Used by permission.

THE AMAZING GROWTH OF JESUS MUSIC IN 1975 CONTINUED ALL OVER the country in 1976, as Jimmy Carter introduced Americans to the term "born again." Virtually unknown before his presidential candidacy, Carter testified to his faith, and brought about a new interest in evangelicalism. In the tradition of *Look* magazine, whose writers in the early '70s had invented the term "Jesus Movement," the press labeled this new consciousness the "Born-Again Movement." Plenty of Christians already knew the meaning of the term, but it was new to people outside the church.

Well-known personalities began verbalizing their faith in Christ as Savior, and in many cases, following dramatic changes in their lives: Chuck Colson and Jeb Stuart Magruder of Watergate infamy; Susan Atkins and Charles "Tex" Watson of the convicted Manson Family; actor Dean Jones of Walt Disney fame; actress Lulu Roman of "Hee Haw"; Eldridge Cleaver of the Black Panthers; and Roger Staubach of the Dallas Cowboys.

The same renewal seemed to be taking place in the musical entertainment field. Singers who once rocked and rolled for fame and fortune changed their tune as they got a better grip on their lives. Though there seemed to be a rash of such testimonies in the late '70s, the changed lives had been occurring throughout the rock and roll years. But it wasn't as easy in the earlier years for entertainers to admit publicly that they were Christians. During the '60s, the popular trend of youth was away from the churches, the Christian religion, and from Americanism. For an artist to declare "I am a Christian," was a bold move with plenty of complications for his or her public life.

Pat Boone was one of the first rock performers to proclaim Christ when it wasn't the popular thing to do. He was chided by critics as being square, milquetoast, the epitome of blandness—yet the number of lives positively affected by Pat Boone's work and witness was definitely nothing to scoff at.

Frequent visits on national television talk shows were an excellent example of this witness. He was not pompous with his religion, and prior to each show, he would carefully pray and ask the Lord whether it was the time and place to speak of Christ verbally, or whether it was more important for him to be a *living* example, while sparing words.

Because between 1955 and 1969, 58 of Pat's records reached the top 100 charts, *Rolling Stone* featured a cover story on Pat in their January 29, 1976 issue. Author John Anderson stated that he had expected Boone to be a "Rasputin-like character." By the conclusion, Anderson mused that he had not found Pat to be the "greedy, money-grabbing hypocrite" he had set out to discover: "Whatever Pat does, He does in response to the voice which calls out to him with a reality he can bank on."[1]

In 1972, Pat formed his own record company, Lamb and Lion Records, on which numerous gospel music and Jesus music performers were given their starts. The work Pat has done in getting the word out about Jesus has been unparalleled by any other pop entertainer.

Pat's daughter Debby carried on a family tradition of hits when she recorded "You Light Up My Life" in 1977. The song became the biggest pop record hit in twenty-three years, and remained in the number 1 position for ten weeks. "You Light Up My Life" had a special meaning for the 21-year-old Debby. The song was the theme from a movie, which she admits she "didn't even agree with." (*Her* recording was not in the movie, nor did she see the movie until after "You Light Up My Life" was #1).

"I sang it to the Lord, and that's all!" she added. "The first time I heard the song, I thought it was just an okay song. But, then when I started listening to the words and saw how it really applied to my relationship with the Lord, then the excitement came!"

With the hit came Debby's opportunity to perform on "The Tonight Show," plus an endless string of other network shows. On such occasions, Debby didn't hide the fact that she was a Christian, especially if the question came up in an interview situation. But she didn't tout her faith on every stage on which she performed. She viewed her function in the Lord's work as being something similar to that of the Ark of the Covenant in the Old Testament—that is, a container of the Holy Spirit.

"I should just be who I am. Debby Boone—container of the Holy Spirit. I don't have to get in a 'good one for the Lord' each time I appear on a TV show. The Power of the Holy Spirit will come across and it will do the work! I don't try to hide it, but I don't try to force it, either. It's just amazing when I get a letter from someone who says, 'I heard your song on the radio and recommitted my life to the Lord,' or 'I was going through such a difficult time in my life and I heard that song and it pulled me through.' And *I* wasn't even trying! I was just singing to the Lord!''

Debby's faith in the Lord was no secret. Nor was that of her three sisters—Laury, Lindy, and Cherry—with whom she recorded Jesus music albums on her father's record label. The sisters' upbringing in a Christian atmosphere made the Boone family the object of heavy scrutiny from the sensationalist press, ready to pounce on them for any wandering from that faith or its life style. But each of the daughters, along with parents Pat and Shirley, withstood such criticism and continued to be strong in their Christian witness.

While John Lennon, Paul McCartney, and George Harrison were singing as "The Quarrymen" in church hall dances and "beat clubs," another young man named Harry Webb made his first record. In August of 1958, Webb took on the professional name of Cliff Richard, and with his group The Drifters, recorded "Move It" and "Schoolboy Crush." The records catapulted Cliff Richard into national prominence as a rock singer.

The hits continued, at a rate of about five a year, and Cliff Richard became Britain's top performer. Even when the Beatles exploded with their hits in the early 1960s, Cliff continued his hold on the charts of Britain, as well as in Europe and Asia.

Thus, in 1966, when Cliff stepped up to the microphone on Billy Graham's podium at a London Crusade where over 25,000 people were present, the whole nation listened. Though he was one of the nation's best-known and most popular individuals, he was nervous.

"I have never had the opportunity to speak to an audience as big as this before," he began, "but it is a great privilege to be able to tell so many people that I am a Christian. I can only say to people who are not Christians that until you have taken the step of asking Christ into your life, your life is not really worthwhile. It *works*—it works for me." [2]

Cliff's announcement hit the pages of every London paper the next morning. Would he end his career and go into "religion"? Just what would become of Cliff Richard was the gossip of the music papers. In a 1972 *Rolling Stone* interview, some four years after his public profession, Cliff expressed a frustration he shared with many other Christians. "When I came out for Jesus, most people said, 'Well there goes a good career,' When it didn't end, they said, 'Oh what a gimmick.' " [3]

Cliff also said in the interview that he challenged the " 'popularity' of Jesus Christ and some of his (Cliff's) contemporaries for going along with it." Cliff added:

> Everybody (is) able to record "My Sweet Lord" and "Oh Happy Day," except me. If I did anything like that everybody would say: "Oh here comes the religious bit." But everybody else could do it. As a Christian I felt that where they all missed out, although they were great records, was that they didn't know exactly who Jesus was. [4]

In 1976, rock superstar Elton John signed Cliff to a contract with his Rocket Record Company. Cliff recorded "Devil Woman" and the song reached #6 on the *Billboard* charts, the biggest American hit of his nineteen-year recording career. Those people who remembered Cliff's statements of his faith back in 1966 were taken aback by such a song as "Devil Woman." Cliff defended the song, stating that it was a warning against occult practices rather than an endorsement.

Cliff's continued testimonies for Christ in pop concerts around the world at least indicated his strong faith. His popularity as a singer enabled Cliff to experience awesome opportunities at witnessing. Not long after his American hit, Cliff was sharing Christ with nearly 70,000 people in—of all places—Leningrad and Moscow.

Noel Paul Stookey met Jesus in an Austin, Texas, motel room. Stookey had been touring for years as the "Paul and" of Peter, Paul & Mary, one of the top vocal groups in the United States during the troubled 1960s. Noel's success as a performer had failed to give him the satisfaction of being a whole person. His friend Bob Dylan had advised him to read the Bible, so Noel was somewhat ready when a young man came up to him at an Austin concert to talk to him about Jesus.

"We got to rapping," Noel recalls. "I had been reading the New Testament and looking for some kind of a moral way to live my life—something more fulfilling than what I had. I had no idea I was gonna get 'smote!'

"It was terrific. I went back to my hotel room and I asked Jesus to come into my life. I cried, and oh! what a fantastic time we had that night! It was just a very cleansing experience." [5]

Noel's acceptance of Christ as Savior led to the dissolution of the Peter, Paul and Mary trio after ten years of many hits together. The three were still friends, but Noel felt it was time.

"I began to see my life as a paradox. I mean, I loved being on the road in terms of the people I met. I was talking about love, togetherness, home and family, and continuity of spirit, but I wasn't living it, because I was on the road four days out of the week. I had a child in school and it just seemed logical after accepting Christ and reading the New Testament that I should get me back to where I belonged." [6]

Noel did just that. He ultimately moved himself and his family to South Blue Hill, Maine (population 1200). He began singing in the Congregational Church Choir. His twin daughters and older daughter began to see more of their father than most musicians' kids. Noel's wife, Elizabeth, took up operation of a greenhouse, and the whole family benefited from Noel's revelation of "how much better it is to live near God."

Noel didn't say farewell to recording, however. He began his own eight-track recording studio and animation studio (he's a cartoonist, too). In 1977, he began releasing albums on his own Neworld label.

In 1978, Noel announced that Peter Yarrow, Mary Travers, and he would reunite as Peter, Paul & Mary for a concert tour and a new recording.

By late 1975, B. J. Thomas' record sales had reached 32 million copies. He scored high with "(Hey Won't You Play) Another Somebody Done Somebody Wrong Song" in early 1975. The singalong hit reached #1.

But just while everything seemed rosy for B. J. in the eyes of the record-buying world, the bottom had fallen out for him. He was a drug addict; his cocaine alone cost $3,000 a week. He was separated from his wife and daughter and could hardly get through a recording session because of his incoherency. He developed a reputation among musicians as being extremely hard to work with and creating havoc in the studios.

"In 1975 I began to realize that I was either going to die or I was going to make a decision to put the drugs down," B. J. recalls. "I couldn't put them down, so I resigned myself to the fact that I was going to eventually kill myself. On many occasions, I would take over 50 pills at one time and I would say 'B., this is going to kill you.' And then I would say, 'Well, who cares?' "

Later in the year, B. J. was scheduled to do a concert in Hawaii. After taking more than 80 pills that particular night, B. J. told the audience he couldn't sing. He left the stage and went back to his hotel room.

"Somehow," B. J. explains, "my road man got me to the airport. They noticed I wasn't breathing very much. My fingernails turned black and my lips turned black. Then, as I got worse, they put a mirror under my nose and couldn't get any breath. For all intents and purposes I had died."

They got B. J. to a hospital and immediately hooked his body up to machines in an effort to revive him. "I woke up the next day and asked them, 'Well, how close was it?' They said I had been gone. Only the machines kept me alive."

Coincidentally, B. J.'s record company had released another single off of his current album. The title, "Help Me Make It (To My Rocking Chair)," said more than anyone on the outside world could imagine.

B. J.'s wife Gloria kept imploring him to come home. Gloria had become a Christian, and she saw light at the end of the tunnel for her husband. By early 1976, he was no more than a hollowed out shell of a man. He finally conceded to return home to Hurst, Texas.

Shortly after he came back, Gloria's witness, his daughter Paige's love, and some friends' prayers led B. J. to accept new life in Christ. He was healed of his drug habit in those intense moments that night in January, 1976. "It was such a miraculous thing for me," he later recalled. "When I received the Lord as my Savior, I just knew I was gonna go through some withdrawals. I knew I was gonna lose my mind. But, I never had one shaky moment, one sleepless night. Nothing bad ever happened."

The next few months were spent pulling his family back together, straightening out finances (including declaring bankruptcy), and generally making plans for a new future. B. J.'s contract with his record label was terminated, and one of his first moves was to do an album of songs relating his love for Christ.

"I just wanted to cut Christian music, but I think that happens so many times with new Christians. If they have a certain career going, they think that God wants them to quit it and do only religious things. I talked to my pastor about it, and he reminded me that a lot of people's ministry is not in a church. I began to realize that if I would just give my testimony at the end of my show, and just as God would have me say it, what a ministry that was!"

So B. J. signed with Myrrh Records to record Christian music, but he also secured a contract with MCA Records to continue singing pop music, too. His first Myrrh album became one of gospel music's all-time best-selling albums, and his first post-Christian pop single, "Don't Worry Baby," became #17 in the nation in 1977.

B. J. had become a *true* success. Not by his 32 million-plus records, he would remind you. It was his yielding to Jesus Christ that gave him a new lease on life. Like other big-name entertainers, he became stronger in Christ, but his strength would continue to be taxed as he ministered in the world and to the world. His entire life became a stage and people were watching every move.

Along with the new "acceptability" of Christianity, Christian music began to flourish at an even more astounding rate in 1977. The world was beginning to take more notice of the music as a result of increased product, promotion, publicity, and the people's genuine search for spiritual values in their lives.

An aggressive push by Christian record companies finally began to get record albums to the *front* of Christian bookstores instead of "back behind the greeting cards." Some Christian bookstores became known as "book and record stores," and the public responded by visiting them more often.

Likewise, the availability of good Jesus music albums increased at an amazing rate. At Word, Incorporated, in 1975 about 5 percent of the recorded product sold was contemporary. Only three years later, the amount had increased to 60 percent.

As record companies began producing more product, more radio stations were able to go on the air with full-time contemporary Christian music—stations such as WINQ in Tampa/St. Petersburg,

KBRN in Brighton/Denver, KFKZ in Greeley/Ft. Collins, KQLH in San Bernardino, KBIQ in Seattle, WYCA in Hammond/Chicago, and numerous others who joined the Jesus music radio pioneers. There were more and more newspapers and magazines giving attention to contemporary Christian music, too. *Gospel Trade, Singing News, Harmony, Cashbox, Record World, Billboard,* and *Contemporary Christian Music* all featured articles and charts on Jesus music.

In 1977, Myrrh Records kicked off a sales promotion campaign which would bring Jesus music into greater prominence than ever before. The $75,000 campaign was run with all the noise and glamor of a movie premiere in Hollywood. Giant posters, sample records in magazines, radio commercials, and special displays prompted Christian book and record store operators to carry more Jesus music. "The music is today, the message is forever" the banners announced. It was Jesus music's biggest advertising boost in its nine-year history.

By the time of the Myrrh campaign, the label had the largest roster of contemporary Christian artists in the country, including many musicians who had been major contributors to Jesus music's history: Malcolm & Alwyn (two of the first British contributors); Michael Omartian (respected Hollywood record producer and keyboard artist); B. J. Thomas; Honeytree; the 2nd Chapter of Acts; the Pat Terry Group; Randy Matthews; Limpic & Rayburn; Bob Ayala; Chris Christian; comedian Mike Warnke (more or less the chaplain of the Jesus music world); David Meece; Lilly Green; and several other artists and groups. Myrrh and the labels distributed under its banner provided some of the best opportunities for musicians to communicate the gospel via Jesus music on record.

Myrrh also distributed several independent labels' recordings: Solid Rock (Larry Norman's label); New Song (Love Inn's label); Good News (pioneer Jesus music label); Messianic (Lamb's label); and Seed (Paul Clark's label). Word, Myrrh's parent company, also distributed a good deal of Jesus music on Light, Lamb & Lion and NewPax Records. Even the more traditional Word label fared well with contemporary Christian music fans through artist Evie Tornquist. Evie's music, like that of the Imperials and Andrae Crouch, tended to break down the barriers between "traditional," "inspirational," and "contemporary"

Christian music. Some people of all ages found some of their music uplifting and enjoyable.

Word, Incorporated was not the only company pushing hard to promote Jesus music. Billy Ray Hearn, who had been with Myrrh Records since its inception, had left Myrrh and Texas to begin the new Sparrow record label in California. Most notable of Sparrow's early releases was Keith Green's first album, *For Him Who Has Ears to Hear*, which became one of the top three contemporary religious albums in 1977 and 1978. Also joining the Sparrow roster were Annie Herring, brothers John and Terry Talbot, Barry McGuire, Janny Grine, Danniebelle Hall, the 2nd Chapter of Acts and Scott Wesley Brown. Sparrow also distributed Birdwing, Spirit, and Neworld Records.

In Nashville, Benson Publishing Company, whose Impact label had reintroduced Larry Norman's *Upon This Rock* and other albums to Jesus music fans in earlier years, had reentered the contemporary music scene via Greentree Records in 1976. By 1978, their release schedule picked up radically, with everything from Reba Rambo Gardner's Streisand-style albums to Dony and Joy McGuire's Christian disco music. Greentree also released albums by Tim Sheppard, Dallas Holm & Praise, and others.

In Kansas City, Tempo started a contemporary label, Chrism, featuring music by long-time Jesus music group, the Hope of Glory. In Pasadena, Texas, Star Song Records was born. In Costa Mesa, California, Maranatha! Music continued adding more artists to its roster. Likewise, other independent labels began springing up all across the country, providing more and more Jesus music for the masses. Jesus music fans had never had it so good.

Part II

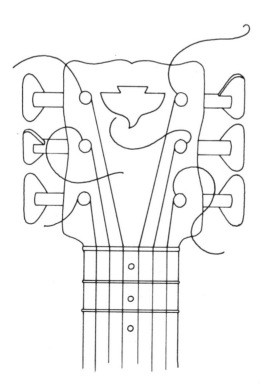

Part II

15/

"We Need a Whole Lot More of Jesus and a Lot Less Rock and Roll"

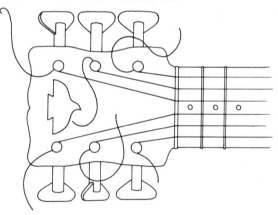

Well you can read it in the morning paper
Hear it on the radio
Crime is sweeping the nation
And the world's about to go
We need a good ole case of salvation
To put the Love of God in our souls
We need a whole lot more of Jesus
And a lot less rock and roll.

We need more old time camp meetings
I said a lot more prayers of faith
Prayers that will move a mountain
And save a soul from burnin' waste
We need a good ole case of salvation
To put the Love of God in our souls
We need a whole lot more of Jesus
And a lot less rock and roll.

THE SUMMER SUN WAS TAKING ITS TOLL IN DENVER. THE MOUNTAINS disappeared into a smoggy atmosphere reminiscent of Los Angeles, and Denver residents apologized, saying it was not usually so bad. I had longed for the weekend when I could head for the mountain peaks and breathe in some cooler and more refreshing air.

I stayed in the Denver area for a few days in July of 1978 to reminisce with Tom Stipe and Danny Taylor about the past eight years or so—where Jesus music had been and where it was going. I'll never forget our enjoyable conversations at Tom's home in Boulder and at the park high in the Rocky Mountains where we picnicked. Much of what was discussed in those hours has been shared in the earlier chapters of this book.

During one of those afternoons in Colorado, Danny, Tom and I had lunch with Evangelist Bob Larson, whose headquarters are in Denver. Bob's reputation had been that of a notorious antirock preacher who broke and burned rock record albums by the hundreds during his crusades. His books were no doubt the objects of burnings themselves by some devotees of rock music.

We were invited to lunch with Bob and his wife at a restaurant on the outskirts of Denver. Thousands of questions were bubbling inside, as the three of us wanted so much to get to know this evangelist who had been so vocal in years past concerning rock music—including Jesus rock music.

Bob told us of his ministry of spiritual warfare. In his crusades around the world, Bob speaks on the sinfulness of the occult, drugs, and numerous other pastimes and practices. He is an outspoken preacher, pulling no punches in delivering warnings to his audiences of the sins of the world.

Because of his outspokenness on so many subjects popular to the world (yoga, drugs, marijuana, alcoholism, pornography, and the occult, as well as many others), Bob explains that he has what he calls a "lonely ministry." That description especially applies to his views on rock music.

But talking to the Bob Larson of today and reading the Bob Larson books of the early '70s are two different matters in many respects.

"The book *Rock and the Church* should be looked at in the proper perspective," Bob explained to us. "When it was written, and even now, my stand on rock music was not a major part of my ministry. It is one night's sermon in a week crusade. But people like to categorize someone and simplify his personality into what they want. With me, it was my preaching on rock music.''

Of course, Bob's earliest books were all to some degree devoted to his views of rock music: *Rock & Roll: The Devil's Diversion* (1967), *Rock and the Church* (1971), *Hippies, Hindus and Rock & Roll* (1970), and *The Day the Music Died* (1973). After 1973, Larson's books centered on other subjects, but the scar remained to be healed.

Referring to *Rock and the Church*, Bob told us, ''The tone of the book was very defensive, and to a certain extent condemnatory, because I was a young preacher, and I was emotionally involved. I hadn't been out of rock music long myself.'' (Larson had been a pop musician before becoming a minister).

''Also,'' he continued, ''I did not know the state of church music, because I had not come out of a church background. So, I did not know how truly archaic it was.''

Jesus musicians who plodded through the last eight years to spread the gospel were greatly upset at any ministry which would seek to destroy what they were convinced the Lord had wanted them to build. So Bob Larson was seen as a man making money off antirock books, and very little more.

''*Rock and the Church* was written in 1971,'' explained Bob. ''That was before there were any Jesus music groups. There's hardly a day that goes by in which someone doesn't write to me and lash out at me for my anti-Jesus music views. The first thing I ask them is, 'Did you see when the book was written?' I ask them to put the book into historical perspective.

''In *Rock and the Church*, I was criticizing the shallow, superficial attempts at copying the sound of the world's music in some sort of vague frame of reference. The book was written before I knew of Love Song, the 2nd Chapter of Acts, and other more solid musicians like that. I did not perceive that a truly authentic and spiritually mature statement of faith and expression of faith would come out of the contemporary field. All I saw was a copy of what the world was doing.

''The second point I try to make to those readers of *Rock and the Church* is to read for basic principles. I still stand by many of its principles today. But the music has matured to a depth that I would not have ever anticipated. What *has* developed in some quarters is an authentic idiom that isn't just a copy of the world. The one thing that does impress me, is even though I still find some musical elements objectionable, the lyrics are not of the sort of throbbing substance they originally were. They now really say something of depth. The change has come from musicians who developed their talents as Jesus musicians, not older musicians trying to copy the sound of the young. In the past six to eight years, musicians have developed Jesus music which is saying some profound things.''

But Bob cautions that his comments do not indicate a blanket endorsement of all Jesus music, and certainly not all rock music. He believes that a rock beat can be a dangerous thing, when it brings with it erotic response or even mental response.

''I still believe that music has the power to transcend one to a spirit plane, and the really super heavy stuff I see as portending that possibility, to the extent that I don't think the Holy Spirit is pleased with being expressed in that frame of reference. That's obviously a subjective line that I'm drawing, but I'm still drawing some lines.''

Bob had picked up a copy of an album by Maranatha Jesus music group Bethlehem, and was especially impressed by a song entitled ''Dead Reckoning,'' one of the hardest rock selections on their album. ''There's an example of a song that musically I don't feel comfortable with, not totally. I can understand why that sort of hard, raunchy style had to be used, because the sort of spiritual sarcasm they're using in speaking to the old man does fit it. I agree that the whole mood created is necessary to an extent. But, if it had been me producing the album, I would have laid it back. But, I think the song does prove a point. In other words, musically it doesn't fit into my frame of reference. But the message is so deep, it has to be genuinely born of the Holy Spirit.''

Bob then cited instances when certain Jesus music songs have been instrumental in even *his* work with people. He cited the Pat Terry Group's song, ''I Feel Free'' as an example. The lyrics of the song helped in Bob's ministry with a woman heavily into witchcraft. He recounts with joy the anointing that song carried.

In another instance, he remembers how ''Abraham,'' a song written by Buck and Annie Herring and recorded by Phil Keaggy on the album *Love Broke Thru,* likewise ministered to a person with whom Bob was counseling. "That particular individual had been involved in the occult. The Lord used the song in a supernatural way to show us the steps we needed to take in our counseling procedure."

"There are two things I look for in any Christian song;" Bob added, "the motive behind it and the ultimate intent. Some of the earliest forms of Jesus music were only meant to be entertaining."

I asked what advice Bob would give to aspiring Jesus musicians. He replied, "I would tell them to let the Holy Spirit do something unique and authentic through them, that would be born of the Holy Spirit, and that it would genuinely say something that would cause reflecting and rejoicing."

Finally, I asked Bob about the current explosion of popular Jesus music artists, with some almost reaching a superstar status among Jesus music fans. Is he fearful that it would get out of hand?

"I am just as fearful as ever," he answered. "It's a natural evolution, bound to happen. I'm very disturbed by the commercial overtones of it all. My advice to any 'fan' of any Christian music would be to read Psalm 101:6. 'My eyes shall be upon the faithful of the land, that they may dwell with me; he who walks in a blameless way is the one who will minister to me.' "

Bob informed us that his next book, *Raising Children in the Rock Generation,* would give parents positive ways to prevent their youth from selling out totally to rock music. "I want to give parents positive ways to handle it, other than going in and smashing all of their kids' records."

One of those positive ways which Bob suggests is through "Jesus music which genuinely glorifies Christ."

16/

"Gospel Light"

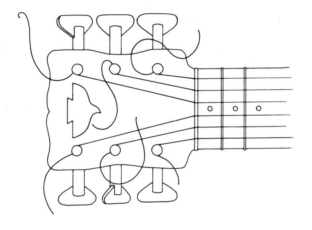

Too many brothers and too many
  sisters seem to grow so weak
When it's time to sing that old
  salvation song
Though there may be someone
  standin' there
Who needs to hear him speak
They just lower their voice, and
  slowly mosey on
Well, I'm glad things didn't
  go that way upon Calvary
And at the last minute, Jesus
  didn't lose His nerve
No He went on to do what
  He had to do
And that's what He expects of you
  and me
Yeah, we've got no choice/but to
  go and spread the word
Stand up and be counted
You will be heard above the noise
If you'll boldly shout it
Sing with your own voice
And don't you be afraid to say it
Don't you try to hide that candle it's
Burnin' in that word you're feelin' inside
It's that gospel light

1978. Thirteen years since Ralph Carmichael's song "He's Everything to Me," set the Christian music world alight.

Ten years since Baptist preacher Arthur Blessitt opened "His Place" at 8428 Sunset Strip to reach out to the runaways, dopers, alcoholics and lonely people.

Nine years since "Oh Happy Day" put Jesus on the charts.

The gigantic Jesus festivals were held for another year: "Jesus '78" in Florida, Pennsylvania, and Ontario; "Fishnet '78" in Virginia; a tremendously successful "Jesus Northwest" festival in Oregon; and, scores of other, smaller events which drew people together in fellowship. Not so small was the Fourth Annual Christian Artists' Music Seminar in the Rockies, more elaborate than ever as the guest roster grew to new lengths and more people planned their summer vacations around the Estes Park camp and the nightly concerts.

It was a sort of "two steps forward, one step back" year for contemporary Christian radio, with five top contemporary stations dropping their Jesus music airplay to assume other formats. That in itself left several cities without a contemporary Christian voice.

However, all the radio news wasn't bad. The number of stations playing at least some contemporary music increased. Likewise, more and more independently produced, syndicated Jesus music radio shows were initiated, providing decent Sunday programming for the thousands of secular radio stations in America.

It was also a year of shifting. The Larry Black Show moved from Freeville to Nashville, Jerry Bryant moved his "Jesus-Solid Rock" from Carbondale to California, Dale Yancy's "Rock That Never Rolls" rolled from Vermont to New York, and "A Joyful Noise" was transferred from Texas to Colorado.

With the widely expanded variety of Christian music, the distinctions between "Jesus music" and other contemporary Christian music had all but faded. Ralph Carmichael, in a magazine article, tried to explain the different types of Christian music and came up with eleven. Traditional artists began recording more contemporary songs just as the secular "traditional" artists had done at least fifteen years earlier. Even singers such as Tennessee Ernie Ford and Ray Price were recording songs by Randy Stonehill and Pat Terry.

Also noticeable around 1978, was a tremendous improvement in the quality of Jesus music recordings. The world had seen Christian music as music of poor quality, and a lot of Christian recordings had provided ample fuel for that fire. Some well-meaning Christians who wanted to jump from knowing four guitar chords to having the top album on the charts in one easy step, or those who regardless of their talent wanted to record an album to please their own egos, made a mockery of gospel music. (In fact, the differentiation between "Jesus music" and "gospel music" was originally the result of the Jesus People's desire to create a new and more professional form of gospel music).

But alas, even some of the Jesus musicians fell into the same trap. Often, they would go into a recording studio before they were ready musically and spiritually. The results were albums of inferior quality. However, through their burning desire to "live up to" the standards set by the world's top rock musicians, the contemporary music makers forced the religious record industry to improve their standards of quality.

Budgets were a great part of the problem. While the Elton Johns of the world had recording budgets in the $100,000 figures, Jesus musicians were lucky to get more than $10,000. A record company could sell a million copies of an Elton John album even before its release, and recoup the album's entire production budget overnight. The Christian record companies would have to wait for a year or so to recover even the lowest of expenditures.

It is possible that the artists who recorded albums of Jesus music were "pressured" into being better artists through working under extremely modest budget conditions, and thus completing albums in considerably less time than their secular counterparts. This extra pressure under which the Jesus musicians worked may have purified their music in some cases.

Through all this recording activity developed a strange irony. Christian musicians and record companies, when producing their albums, began hiring top studio musicians—the same ones who appeared on hundreds of pop recordings each year. The combination of a talented artist or group, a competent producer, and expert studio musicians, would often yield a top-notch recording—one not only compatible with the top pop hits, but sometimes even better. After all, numerous Jesus music artists had had #1 secular hits and million-selling records. In fact, they had totalled way over 13 #1 hits, and probably over 200 million records! Yet, the Jesus music songs by these same artists (by no means has-beens), done in the same studios, performed by virtually the same musicians, and often written by the same people, never even touched the top hit charts in America! The problem still exists.

Prejudice against religion hardly seems a justifiable reason for the pop music world to turn down fine music by fine musicians. But prejudice *is* a main reason. The Bible makes it very clear that the world will not necessarily look on the Christians (or their music) with favor. "For unto them the preaching of the cross is foolishness, but unto us who believe it is the power of salvation." [1]

The Jesus musicians' challenge to the world's prejudice is the added dimension which contemporary Christian music offers. It is mainstream rock music, on par with many of the world's hits. It is music which, without being overly preachy, is uplifting and positive. It is music with answers, not problems. Hope, not despair. Love, not lust. Life, not death. The twentieth century world has never seen, heard or experienced anything like it.

There is an awesome responsibility before those people involved in contemporary Christian music. Their music must be professional and something the world will listen to, but it must exude the Truth with every word. That obviously doesn't mean each song must have "Jesus saved me, this I know" repeated over and over. It *does* mean, however, that each song should be conceived, written, performed, and recorded under absolute direction of the Holy Spirit. Christian musicians and their record companies must be cautious not to compromise their music to get it into the secular marketplace.

With the extremely rapid growth of Jesus music, the momentum has occasionally bordered on frenzy. Vestiges of the world's star-oriented society creep into the promotion of Jesus music artists. Madison Avenue-type ads describing so-and-so as "a new star in gospel music" border on the outer limits of where Jesus music should go. In fact, such promotion prompted one group to print T-shirts with the message "Jesus Christ is the only star." They're seeking to reestablish priorities.

There has always been a secret dream of Jesus music fans to see one of the artists break through the national charts with a giant "Jesus hit." Plenty of musicians have set that as their personal goal, too. But it shows a limited knowledge of how God can work.

We've seen *Jesus Christ Superstar* and *Godspell* ignite controversy and popularize the man Jesus at the same time. Some

190 # Why Should the Devil Have All the Good Music?

Christians recall how *Superstar* first interested them in Jesus—others are still repulsed at the brazenness of the production. *Godspell* entertained millions of people, but no one can tell how many people became Christians as a result of enjoying the play or movie.

"Put Your Hand in the Hand," "Jubilation," "Jesus Is Just Alright," "Jesus Is a Soul Man"—all of the big Jesus hits of the seventies may have kept making Jesus "impressions" on the minds of the hearers, but they didn't bring the country to repentance.

What *has* made the difference has been Jesus music teamed up with a critical ingredient—witness. The big Top 40 Jesus hits were recorded mainly as a part of the "fad" created by the Jesus Movement. It was "in" to sing about Jesus. Thus, there were hits.

But the *real* Jesus music most often has been the music by the non-"stars". Music by minstrels whose daily bread was often their only pay. Music by singers whom nobody understood, but who believed in what they were doing for the Lord. Singers who traveled tens of thousands of miles while their spouses sat at home missing them. Musicians whose love for their Heavenly Father stripped away any star-image they might have when they publicly cried on stage in response to what the Lord had done for them.

The living witnesses of the musicians speak as loudly as any of the songs they sing. Debby Boone's testimony of her faith in God spoke clearly to all the fans of her smash hit, "You Light Up My Life." B. J. Thomas' vivid witness in each of his pop concerts *spoke* of the Lord to the audiences. The witness of Christian musicians must be as strong and as important as their music. The public watches and hears both.

So, perhaps in God's infinite wisdom he does not see the necessity of putting a Christian artist with a Jesus song at the top of the charts. The Lord can use stars. He can also use unknowns. The Lord can even use has-beens in His work. But a musician should never strive for being anything else than what his Lord wants him to be. The goal should never be to be a "star" for Jesus unless the person is already a star. Gaining "star" status brings with it inherent problems. Personalities change, priorities change, purposes change. The performer's goals should be to please the Father, whether it be singing in one-night stands, or appearing on national television. For, as one Scripture proclaims, "Promotion comes neither from the east, nor from the west, nor from the south. But God is the judge: he puts down one, and exalts another." [2]

Epilogue

DURING THREE AUGUST DAYS IN 1978, THE FELLOWSHIP OF CONTEMporary Christian Ministries had its third annual retreat, this time in the wooded environs of the Agape Force Ranch near Lindale, Texas. Since the FCCM's formation with charter members in 1975, the membership had grown to more than 350.

Following the three days of fellowship and worship, the topic of discussion was "Where is Jesus music headed?" "What's the next step?" Talks by ministers Tony Salerno and Winkie Pratney had been calls for a return to holiness for all Christians.

One of the people who privately shared his thoughts on the subject was Terry Talbot. In the late 1960s, Terry and his brother John had performed as secular rock musicians in the group Mason Proffit, who had an excellent following through their numerous albums. In 1974, the liner notes on their album *The Talbot Brothers* gave hints of their new faith in Christ. Two years later, both of them began recording Christian albums for Sparrow Records.

My wife Debbie and I joined Terry on the porch of the guest house, seeking some relief from the sweltering August sun. I asked Terry how Jesus music and the Jesus Movement had affected him over the past ten years.

"For those of us who were not involved in it," Terry replied, "the Jesus Movement was incredibly small. When I was in the world, I didn't know anything about it or the music. The whole thing to me was a bunch of kids in California who went to the beach every Sunday to be photographed by *Time* magazine. That's all I knew about it. It amazes me in retrospect that that's all we nonbelievers heard about it. I know it was magnificent to be a part of it, but that magnificence never reached me or a lot of other people."

As Terry recounted how small the Movement seemed back then, I recalled the startling number of people I had recently talked to who never even opened a Bible or read a Bible verse until they were well into their twenties. It's so easy to fall into a trap of believing *everyone* knows about the Bible if you do yourself. The truth is, they don't.

"Where were you in 1969 when the Jesus Movement was really starting?" I asked.

"We were cutting the first Mason Proffit album."

"None of you were Christians then?"

"No," he replied. "We were brought up in church and I would defend Jesus philosophically to anyone who thought another way was better. I always knew He was the only way, but I didn't know any way to walk with the Lord. I didn't know how.

"When I first came to the Lord, when I was on the road with the Eagles, I still had never heard of the 2nd Chapter of Acts or Larry Norman or Word Records or any of that. And that was only a few years ago! The thing that's amazing to me is that John and I were doing what all of these young Jesus musicians are trying so hard to do! 'Let's go out there, get on a secular concert bill. Then, let's go for it and preach the gospel.'

"That's all we *knew* to do! You make a record and do a tour with a major group and you go for it. We'd never heard of all this. We didn't know that Jesus music was called that! It was just more of our music!

"Then I began to hear Jesus music, and to be quite honest, I wasn't real impressed with it. But the Lord dealt with me on that, that no matter how bad it was technically, it still blessed the socks off a lot of people.

"Then I heard 'Easter Song' and I got blown away. I just wept when I heard it."

I asked Terry to share his opinions of where Jesus music is headed. He responded by again referring to the early days of the Jesus Movement.

"As the Jesus Movement grew, so did a new danger," he said. "I think of what happened in 1969 and 1970. The Movement was really made up of the salt of the earth. But it seems the salt stayed in the shaker in many ways. The Lord poured more salt in the shaker, and the cap was put on by the church itself in some cases, and most of the holes were plugged up. Nobody turned it upside down and gave it a shake so that we could fall out. And that's what we need now. The church needs a good shake, and it's happening!

"We've become so introspective, so narcistic, that we just turn inward and begin to examine ourselves and stop reaching out. I can remember back before I knew the Lord, I was dying! I *needed* someone to reach out!

"I think we're taking the first step toward a revival," he added. "and a return to a genuine desire to walk with Jesus. I think that there are a lot of people in Christian music who don't belong there.

God is calling them someplace else and they ought to be there to do whatever it is. I think it's gonna get real big real fast and contemporary Christian music is going to be the harp that heralds the end times, the Second Coming.

"David or the musicians would play before the prophets would prophesy. We're in that position. We've taken upon us that office in the body of Christ. So there is that call to a real tight walk with the Lord Jesus. It is heavy! I know in my life right now the Lord is calling me. It's time to take the garbage out and minister, and I don't want to do anything if I don't minister Jesus."

The conversations with Terry Talbot and other seasoned musicians, promoters, broadcasters, even Christian record store operators, have revealed a few disturbing facts. First, there are many people who see the urgent need for renewal within the Jesus music industry. Just the fact that it is called an industry, and the various cities where the musicians play and record their records are now called "markets," exposes far more than some people want to see. The ministry has become a business, and many musicians see their only way of getting to their goals as succumbing to the "system" which is rapidly being defined. For "success" you need to be "popular." To be popular you need "hits." To get hits, you need more "exposure." For exposure, you sign "contracts." Your songs must be "commercial."

In his book, *The Worldly Evangelicals*, Richard Quebedeaux warns that "Historically, since the time of Constantine, whenever the church has become 'established'—too popular, too respectable—corruption and secularism have become rampant within its ranks." [1] This is too important a warning for us to treat lightly, because Jesus music, in fact the entire "contemporary gospel" industry (which has somewhat overshadowed Jesus music lately), is vulnerable in the same way as is the entire evangelical church.

The vulnerability isn't so much a threat that big business will discover Jesus rock and exploit it; they tried it in the early '70s and it lasted only a year or so. The concern should be for a vulnerability from *within* the camp. Priorities can be forgotten in the roar of the crowd. And in many cases, the musician has come to worship and serve the Jesus music rather than Jesus. This attitude has encouraged Jesus music fans to do the same.

Expert musicianship and sketchy training in the Word doth not an excellent witness make. There is a brand new generation of modern-day Christian "minstrels" now "arriving" on the scene. They are stepping into the world of "contemporary Christian music" with no knowledge of the battles fought to keep Jesus music alive during the past ten years, nor any recollection even of why and how Jesus music came about. Meanwhile, the "youth" of the early Jesus Movement are now parents themselves, and I'm sure that it won't be long before even newer and more innovative musical styles will be introduced which will raise *their* eyebrows. Even, heaven forbid, Christian punk rock. (Already certain magazine ads and covers for Christian rock artists feature photographs of the artists in a somber, grimacing mood very similar to those used in promoting secular punk rock groups).

Though the *styles* of the music may shock the fainthearted, they are not the major cause for worry. Leadership is—rather, the lack of it. A great number of the new, potential "ministers" of the Jesus music genre lack any leadership at all—from the churches, but probably worse, even from their peers.

There remains an alarming apathy on the part of many youth ministers and church music ministers to encourage, nourish, and guide the churched or unchurched youth in their chosen line of endeavor, even ministry. Quite frankly, in all too many cases, there is no one in the church to turn to if a young person's interests lie in communicating the gospel through rock music. Either that church categorically denounces rock, or the interpretation of the term "contemporary Christian music" is the stumbling block. The youth minister, music minister or pastor views all "contemporary Christian music" as being large choral groups of twenty or thirty youth, maybe more, singing middle-of-the-road Christian music which in reality communicates mainly to the elder members of the congregation. The young person who sees the validity of a Christian *rock* ministry has a completely different type of music in mind. The difference in interpretation ends there, at a stalemate, and the youth's creativity is quite possibly stifled. A potential "music minister" may thus channel his ambitions and energy elsewhere, though he was receiving a genuine call of the Lord in Jesus music.

Church-oriented ministers *must* begin widening their horizons when it comes to youth and their music. Rock music is *not* going to fade away as many adults predicted and hoped. It's here for a long time, like it or not, and the number of people affected by it is constantly growing. *How* they are affected by it can in many ways be determined by the church. Whether or not rock music is to the liking of the leaders, there *are* ways of using it for the glory of God.

Newcomer Jesus musicians also need the expressed concern and the encouragement of their brothers and sisters in the ministry. In conversation with the more established musicians, I have seen a general lack of interest on the part of the "professionals" when it comes to nurturing the younger musicians and guiding them.

Quite frankly, many of the older Jesus musicians, having been in the "business" for anywhere from four to ten years, are getting tired. Tired of traveling to one-night stands (and trying to keep their families together, too). Tired of leaving behind young audience members who will receive no follow-up after their concert (such as witnessing, invitations to a specific church, or even friendship). Tired of the rejection of their music by so many churches (such as church leaders who never offer the youth of their church a ride on one of their buses to attend a local Jesus music concert, mainly because someone *else* is putting it on). Tired of trying to serve their Lord in music while they see some trite, "plastic gospel" albums with "commercial" value wedge them out of a recording contract.

No wonder they're fatigued! It's been an uphill climb. And ten years later the problems haven't been solved so much as they have been made more complex. Unfortunately, some of the veteran musicians are about to give up, when the victory could be just around the corner, if they would just "press on toward the mark." They are sapped of energy and will, though, and they need renewal.

The tired, established Jesus musicians would probably benefit from a Paul/Timothy relationship with younger musicians. The vitality and the zeal of the young is refreshing, and could well engender a more optimistic view of things. Don't the veterans remember that that same vitality *was* the Jesus movement in the late '60s and early '70s? And far be it for the older ones to *discourage* the younger. Paul, training Timothy for the ministry, *encouraged*: "Let no man despise thy youth, but be thou an example of the believers, in word, in conduct, in love, in spirit, in faith, in purity." [2]

In my work with the Fellowship of Contemporary Christian Ministries, I have received an alarmingly high number of letters from young people wanting advice on their music, their aspirations, and their callings; young people who complain that there is no one who understands them. They are even willing to "submit" themselves as Peter challenged:

"Likewise, ye younger, submit yourselves unto the elder. Yea, all of you be subject one to another, and be clothed with humility: for God resisteth the proud, and giveth grace to the humble. Humble yourselves therefore under the mighty hand of God, that he may exalt you in due time: casting all your care upon him; for he careth for you." [3]

But where are the leaders for these "younger" to turn to? On one hand, the church ministers most often seem too busy to involve themselves with someone or something that does not happen within the total confines of their "church program," and the related lack of compassion, or at least, understanding, is depressing. On the other hand, many of the Jesus musicians are either run down with no real hope, or they are so occupied with their own music and their own work that they are never even aware of what fellow musicians are doing, writing, or feeling; much less do they take time to encourage or exhort the newcomers.

Thank God for the preachers, youth ministers, music ministers, musicians, teachers, parents and others who are taking the time to care—to extend the hand of Christian fellowship to these musicians of the '80s and the '90s. The original strength of the Jesus Movement didn't come from radio, television, records, or magazines. It came from one-to-one confrontation and one-to-one caring. A great number of the Jesus musicians mentioned in this book were won to the Lord by a face-to-face confrontation with one person. For Noel Paul Stookey, it was someone in a motel room following a concert. For Barry McGuire, it was a Jesus freak on a Hollywood street. For B. J. Thomas, it was his wife. The work of individuals, meeting with and having compassion on these performers, changed their direction and indirectly resulted in thousands of people coming to know Christ as Savior. The work of countless young Christian musicians now seeking to begin their ministries will be just as important in the future years.

Though the observations made in this chapter are somewhat negative, the spirit of the early Jesus Movement is still alive today in hundreds of contemporary Christian musicians and likewise in thousands of nonmusicians. The electricity can be felt. Our concern is that this tremendous energy is not stifled.

In its early years, Jesus music was rough on the edges; more or less a jalopy in appearance, but with an extraordinarily dynamic engine within. All the parts worked together quite well, with positive results—especially, countless changed lives.

Contemporary Christian music has come a long way since the jalopy days. Recordings sound more professional, and there are more and more of them available. The Christian bookstore operators, once wary of Jesus music and the musicians themselves, are now carrying complete lines of contemporary Christian music. Radio station programmers are gradually widening the limits of musical styles featured, and more and more secular broadcasting outlets are featuring Jesus music on Sunday mornings. Contemporary gospel albums are showing up more frequently as nominations for Grammy and Dove Award-winners. (The Dove is the gospel counterpart of the Grammy).

But we must make sure that "contemporary gospel," as the industry itself has tagged it, doesn't become a sparkling new show car with a jalopy engine. We've polished the outside until it's starting to gleam, but there is a lot of maintenance on the inside that is being forgotten. Some of the parts of that originally well-tuned engine have become frayed or rusty, through ordinary wear, through misuse, and sometimes through outright neglect. Once we get those inner parts renewed. we'll be truly roadworthy again!

In his book, *The Worldly Evangelicals*, Richard Quebedeaux warns that "Historically, since the time of Constantine, whenever the church has become 'established'—too popular, too respectable—corruption and secularism have become rampant within its ranks." [1] This is too important a warning for us to treat lightly, because Jesus music, in fact the entire "contemporary gospel" industry (which has somewhat overshadowed Jesus music lately), is vulnerable in the same way as is the entire evangelical church.

The vulnerability isn't so much a threat that big business will discover Jesus rock and exploit it; they tried it in the early '70s and it lasted only a year or so. The concern should be for a vulnerability from *within* the camp. Priorities can be forgotten in the roar of the crowd. And in many cases, the musician has come to worship and serve the Jesus music rather than Jesus. This attitude has encouraged Jesus music fans to do the same.

Expert musicianship and sketchy training in the Word doth not an excellent witness make. There is a brand new generation of modern-day Christian "minstrels" now "arriving" on the scene. They are stepping into the world of "contemporary Christian music" with no knowledge of the battles fought to keep Jesus music alive during the past ten years, nor any recollection even of why and how Jesus music came about. Meanwhile, the "youth" of the early Jesus Movement are now parents themselves, and I'm sure that it won't be long before even newer and more innovative musical styles will be introduced which will raise *their* eyebrows. Even, heaven forbid, Christian punk rock. (Already certain magazine ads and covers for Christian rock artists feature photographs of the artists in a somber, grimacing mood very similar to those used in promoting secular punk rock groups).

Though the *styles* of the music may shock the fainthearted, they are not the major cause for worry. Leadership is—rather, the lack of it. A great number of the new, potential "ministers" of the Jesus music genre lack any leadership at all—from the churches, but probably worse, even from their peers.

There remains an alarming apathy on the part of many youth ministers and church music ministers to encourage, nourish, and guide the churched or unchurched youth in their chosen line of endeavor, even ministry. Quite frankly, in all too many cases, there is no one in the church to turn to if a young person's interests lie in communicating the gospel through rock music. Either that church categorically denounces rock, or the interpretation of the term "contemporary Christian music" is the stumbling block. The youth minister, music minister or pastor views all "contemporary Christian music" as being large choral groups of twenty or thirty youth, maybe more, singing middle-of-the-road Christian music which in reality communicates mainly to the elder members of the congregation. The young person who sees the validity of a Christian *rock* ministry has a completely different type of music in mind. The difference in interpretation ends there, at a stalemate, and the youth's creativity is quite possibly stifled. A potential "music minister" may thus channel his ambitions and energy elsewhere, though he was receiving a genuine call of the Lord in Jesus music.

Church-oriented ministers *must* begin widening their horizons when it comes to youth and their music. Rock music is *not* going to fade away as many adults predicted and hoped. It's here for a long time, like it or not, and the number of people affected by it is constantly growing. *How* they are affected by it can in many ways be determined by the church. Whether or not rock music is to the liking of the leaders, there *are* ways of using it for the glory of God.

Newcomer Jesus musicians also need the expressed concern and the encouragement of their brothers and sisters in the ministry. In conversation with the more established musicians, I have seen a general lack of interest on the part of the "professionals" when it comes to nurturing the younger musicians and guiding them.

Quite frankly, many of the older Jesus musicians, having been in the "business" for anywhere from four to ten years, are getting tired. Tired of traveling to one-night stands (and trying to keep their families together, too). Tired of leaving behind young audience members who will receive no follow-up after their concert (such as witnessing, invitations to a specific church, or even friendship). Tired of the rejection of their music by so many churches (such as church leaders who never offer the youth of their church a ride on one of their buses to attend a local Jesus music concert, mainly because someone *else* is putting it on). Tired of trying to serve their Lord in music while they see some trite, "plastic gospel" albums with "commercial" value wedge them out of a recording contract.

No wonder they're fatigued! It's been an uphill climb. And ten years later the problems haven't been solved so much as they have been made more complex. Unfortunately, some of the veteran musicians are about to give up, when the victory could be just around the corner, if they would just "press on toward the mark." They are sapped of energy and will, though, and they need renewal.

The tired, established Jesus musicians would probably benefit from a Paul/Timothy relationship with younger musicians. The vitality and the zeal of the young is refreshing, and could well engender a more optimistic view of things. Don't the veterans remember that that same vitality *was* the Jesus movement in the late '60s and early '70s? And far be it for the older ones to *discourage* the younger. Paul, training Timothy for the ministry, *encouraged*: "Let no man despise thy youth, but be thou an example of the believers, in word, in conduct, in love, in spirit, in faith, in purity." [2]

IT'S TIME WE RETURNED

It was a quiet revolution we had a few years ago
We gave out a sandwich and a Bible to help them grow
And they grew beyond our wildest dreams 'til the nation realized
The kind of Jesus that we talked about and what He could do besides.

And it's time we returned to our call
Otherwise the children gonna fall
And it's time we returned to simplicity
The simple job of settin' people free.

If you stop beside our offices
We've grown in ministry
But we have our appointments
And we have not time to see
The empty, lonely people
That we were placed here for
With some vague sense of purpose
As we rush right out the door.

And it's time we returned to our call
Otherwise the children gonna fall
And it's time we returned to simplicity
The simple job of settin' people free. . . .

—Words and music by Michael C. Johnson
© Copyright 1977 by Paragon Music Corp. Used by permission.

Part III

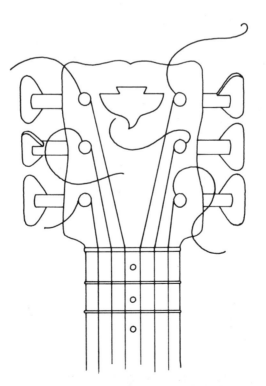

Index of Appendices

Appendix A. "Religious" Songs Which Reached the *Billboard* Top 100 Pop Charts 1955–1978

Appendix B. Hit Songs by Artists Who Also Recorded Jesus Music Albums

Appendix C. A Complete Listing of All Known Jesus Music Recording Artists and the Labels on Which They Have Recorded

Appendix D. Charts: Gospel Music 1964 & Gospel Music 1979

Appendix E. Bibliography and Suggested Reading

Appendix A

Following is a list of songs of a "religious" nature, generally in keeping with Judeo-Christian concepts. Each of the songs appeared on the *Billboard* Top 100 singles charts between 1955—1979. The recording artists listed are not all Christians. Obviously, songs such as "Stairway to Heaven," "Kiss an Angel Good Morning," or "You'll Never Get to Heaven If You Break My Heart" are omitted. Likewise, songs expressing other faiths, such as Seals' and Crofts' "Hummingbird" and George Harrison's "My Sweet Lord," are not included.

Appendix A
"Religious" Songs Which Reached
The *Billboard* Top 100 Pop Charts
1955–1978

1955
Angels in the Sky—*Crew Cuts*—#13—Mercury 70741
Bible Tells Me So—*Don Cornell*—#7—Coral 61467
He—*Al Hibbler*—#7—Decca 29660
He—*McGuire Sisters*—#12—Coral 61494

1956
Every Time (I Feel His Spirit)—*Patti Page*—#87 Mercury 70971
Give Us This Day—*Joni James*—#30—MCM 12288
The Good Book—*Kay Starr*—#89—RCA Victor 47-6617
Sinner Man—*Les Baxter*—#82—Capitol 3404

1957
(There'll Be) Peace in the Valley—*Elvis Presley*—#39 RCA Victor EPA 4054
There's a Gold Mine in the Sky—*Pat Boone*—#28—Dot 15602

1958
He's Got the Whole World (In His Hands)—*Laurie London*—#2 Capitol 3891
He's Got the Whole World in His Hands—*Mahalia Jackson*—#69 Columbia 41150

1959
Battle Hymn of the Republic—*Mormon Tabernacle Choir*—#13 Columbia 41459
Deck of Cards—*Wink Martindale*—#7—Dot 15968
When the Saints Go Marching In—*Fats Domino*—#50 Imperial 5569

1960
Wings of a Dove—*Ferlin Husky*—#12—Capitol 4406

1961
Child of God—*Bobby Darin*—#95—Atco 6183
Michael—*Highwaymen*—#1—United Artists 258

1963
Dominique—*The Singing Nun*—#1—Philips 40152
Michael—*Steve Alaimo*—#100—Checker 1054

1964

All My Trials—*Dick & Deedee*—#89—Warner Bros. 5411
Amen—*Impressions*—#7—ABC-Paramount 10602
I Believe—*Bachelors*—#33—London 9672
Oh, Rock My Soul—*Peter, Paul & Mary*—#93—Warner Bros. 5442
Michael—*Trini Lopez*—#42—Reprise 0300
Tell It on the Mountain—*Peter, Paul & Mary*—#33—Warner Bros. 5418
You'll Never Walk Alone—*Patti LaBelle & Blue Belles*—#34 Nicetown 5020 & Parkway
   896

1965

Crying in the Chapel—*Elvis Presley*—#3—RCA Victor 447-0643
Crying in the Chapel—*Adam Wade*—#88—Epic 9752
People Get Ready—*Impressions*—#14—ABC-Paramount 10622
Sinner Man—*Trini Lopez*—#54—Reprise 0405
Michael—*C.O.D.'s*—#41—Kellmac 1003
Turn! Turn! Turn!—*Byrds*—#1—Columbia 43424
You'll Never Walk Alone—*Gerry & The Pacemakers*—#48 Laurie 3302

1966

He—*Righteous Brothers*—#18—Verve 10406

1967

Get Together—*Youngbloods*—#62—RCA 47-9264

1968

Amen—*Otis Redding*—#36—Atco 6592
Battle Hymn of the Republic—*Andy Williams*—#33 Columbia 44650
Daddy Sang Bass—*Johnny Cash*—#42—Columbia 44689
You'll Never Walk Alone—*Elvis Presley*—#90—RCA Victor 47-9600

1969

Crystal Blue Persuasion—*Tommy James & the Shondells*—#2 Roulette 7050
Dammit Isn't God's Last Name—*Frankie Lane*—#86 ABC 11224
Get Together—*Youngbloods*—#5—RCA 47-9264
Jesus Is a Soul Man—*Lawrence Reynolds*—#28 Warner Bros. 7322
Kum Ba Ya—*Tommy Leonetti*—#54—Decca 32421
Oh Happy Day—*Edwin Hawkins Singers*—#4—Pavilion 20001
Sweet Cherry Wine—*Tommy James & the Shondells*—#7 Roulette 7039
That's the Way God Planned It—*Billy Preston*—#62 Apple 1808
Turn! Turn! Turn!—*Judy Collins*—#69—Elektra 45680
You'll Never Walk Alone—*Brooklyn Bridge*—#51—Buddah 139

1970

Amazing Grace—*Judy Collins*—#15—Elektra 45709
Are You Ready—*Pacific Gas & Electric*—#14—Columbia 45158
Church Street Soul Revival—*Tommy James*—#62—Roulette 7093
Everything Is Beautiful—*Ray Stevens*—#1—Barnaby 2011
Fire and Rain—*James Taylor*—#3—Warner Bros. 7423
Fire and Rain—*R. B. Greaves*—#82—Atco 6745
Fire and Rain—*Johnny Rivers*—#94—Imperial 66453

Chart information taken from Joel Whitburn's Record Research, compiled from Billboard's "Pop" charts.

Holy Man—*Diane Kolby*—#67—1970—Columbia 45169
I Heard the Voice of Jesus—*Turley Richards*—#99—1970 Warner Bros. 7397
Jesus Is Just Alright—*Byrds*—#97—1970—Columbia 45071
Oh Happy Day—*Glen Campbell*—#40—1970—Capitol 2787
Spirit in the Sky—*Norman Greenbaum*—#3—1970—Reprise 0885
Spirit in the Sky—*Dorothy Morrison*—#99—1970—Buddah 196
Stealing in the Name of the Lord—*Paul Kelly*—#49—1970 Happy Tiger 541
Stoned Love—*Supremes*—#7—1970—Motown 1172
Superstar—*Murray Head*—#74—1970—Decca 32603

1971
All My Trials—*Ray Stevens*—#70—Barnaby 2039
Come Back Home—*Bobby Goldsboro*—#69—United Artists 50807
Deep Enough For Me—*Ocean*—#73—Kama Sutra 525
Grandma's Hands—*Bill Withers*—#42—Sussex 227
Life—*Elvis Presley*—#53—RCA 47-9985
Mighty Clouds of Joy—*B. J. Thomas*—#34—Scepter 12320
My Sweet Lord—*Billy Preston*—#90—Apple 1826
Put Your Hand in the Hand—*Ocean*—#2—Kama Sutra 519
Superstar—*Murray Head*—#14—Decca—32603
Take My Hand—*Kenny Rogers & First Edition*—#91 Reprise 1018
Think His Name—*Johnny Rivers*—#65—United Artists 50822
Top 40 of the Lord—*Sha Na Na*—#84—Kama Sutra 528
Turn Your Radio On—*Ray Stevens*—#63—Barnaby 2048
Wedding Song (There Is Love)—*Paul Stookey*—#24 Warner Bros. 7511

1972
Amazing Grace—*Royal Scots Dragoon Guards*—#11 RCA 74-0709
Day By Day—*Godspell*—#13—Bell 45, 210
I'll Take You There—*Staple Singers*—#1—Stax 0125
Jesus Is Just Alright—*Doobie Bros.*—#35—Warner Bros. 7619
Joy—*Apollo 100*—#6—Mega 615-0050
Jubilation—*Paul Anka*—#65—Buddah 294
Me and Jesus—*Tom T. Hall*—#98—Mercury 73278
Morning Has Broken—*Cat Stevens*—#6—A & M 1335
Speak to the Sky—*Rick Springfield*—#14—Capitol 3340
That's The Way God Planned It—*Billy Preston*——#65 Apple 1808
Wedding Song (There Is Love)—*Petula Clark*—#61 MGM 14431
Wholly Holy—*Aretha Franklin*—#81—Atlantic 2901

1973
He—*Today's People*—#90—20th Cent. 2032
I Knew Jesus (Before He Was a Star)—*Glen Campbell*—#45 Capitol 3548
Put Your Hands Together—*O'Jays*—#10—Philadelphia International 3535

1974
City in the Sky—*Staple Singers*—#79—Stax 0215
Lord's Prayer—*Sister Janet Mead*—#4—A & M 1491
There Will Never Be Any Peace (Until God Is Seated at the Conference Table)—*Chi-Lites*—
    #63—Brunswick 55512

Chart information taken from Joel Whitburn's Record Research, compiled from Billboard's "Pop" charts.

1975

L-O-V-E (Love)—*Al Green*—#13—Hi 2282

1976

None

1977

You Light Up My Life—*Debby Boone*—#1—Warner/Curb 8455

1978

Belle—*Al Green*—#83—Hi 77505
Rivers of Babylon—*Boney M.*—#30—Sire Hansa 1027

Chart information taken from Joel Whitburn's Record Research, compiled from Billboard's "Pop" charts.

Appendix B
HIT SONGS BY ARTISTS WHO ALSO RECORDED
JESUS MUSIC ALBUMS

In the following list are the pop record hits by artists who have also recorded albums of Jesus music. This listing does not imply that only those pop musicians included are Christian, nor does the list include recordings on which Jesus musicians played as session men. Such musicians as Michael Omartian, Mike and Kathi Deasy, Noel Stookey, Gary S. Paxton and many more have played on scores of other artists' recordings. It is virtually impossible to make an exhaustive list; thus, this partial list is provided for the enjoyment of the reader.

Debby Boone
1977   "You Light Up My Life" #1
1978   "California" #50
1978   "God Knows"/"Baby, I'm Yours" #74

Pat Boone
1955   "At My Front Door" (Crazy Little Mama)" #7
1955   "No Other Arms" #26
1955   "Gee Whittakers!" #27
1956   "I'll Be Home" #5
1956   "Tutti Fruiti" #12
1956   "Long Tall Sally" #18
1956   "Just As Long As I'm With You" #76
1956   "I Almost Lost My Mind" #1
1956   "I'm In Love With You" #57
1956   "Friendly Persuasion" #8
1956   "Chains of Love" #20
1956   "Don't Forbid Me" #1
1956   "Anastasia" #37
1957   "Why Baby Why" #6
1957   "I'm Waiting Just For You" #27
1957   "Love Letters In The Sand" #1
1957   "Bernardine" #23
1957   "Remember You're Mine" #20
1957   "There's A Gold Mine in the Sky" #28
1957   "April Love" #1
1957   "When the Swallows Come Back to Capistrano" #80
1958   "A Wonderful Time Up There" #10
1958   "It's Too Soon to Know" #13
1958   "Sugar Moon" #11
1958   "Cherie, I Love You" #63
1958   "If Dreams Came True" #12
1958   "That's How Much I Love You" #39
1958   "For My Good Fortune" #23
1958   "Gee, But It's Lonely" #31
1958   "I'll Remember Tonight" #34
1959   "With the Wind and the Rain in Your Hair" #21
1959   "Good Rockin' Tonight" #49

Chart information taken from Joel Whitburn's Record Research, compiled from Billboard's "Pop" charts.

1959	"For A Penny" #23	
1959	"The Wang Dang Taffy Apple Tango" #62	
1959	"Twixt Twelve and Twenty" #17	
1959	"Fool's Hall of Fame" #29	
1959	"Beyond the Sunset" #71	
1960	"(Welcome) New Lovers" #18	
1960	"Words" #94	
1960	"Walking the Floor Over You" #44	
1960	"Spring Rain" #50	
1960	"Delia Gone" #66	
1960	"Candy Sweet" #72	
1960	"Dear John" #44	
1960	"Alabam" #47	
1961	"The Exodus Song" #64	
1961	"Moody River" #1	
1961	"Big Cold Wind" #19	
1961	"Johnny Will" #35	
1962	"I'll See You In My Dreams" #32	
1962	"Pictures in the Fire" #77	
1962	"Quando, Quando, Quando" #95	
1962	"Speedy Gonzales" #6	
1962	"Ten Lonely Guys" #45	
1963	"Meditation" #91	
1964	"Beach Girl" #72	
1966	"Wish You Were Here Buddy" #49	
1969	"July You're A Woman" #100	

Chris Christian
with *Cotton, Lloyd & Christian*
1975   "I Go To Pieces" #66

Jessi Colter
1975   "I'm Not Lisa" #4
1975   "Whatever Happened to Blue Eyes?/You Ain't Never Been Loved" #57

Gene Cotton
1974   "Sunshine Roses" #79
1975   "Damn It All" #73
1976   "You've Got Me Runnin' " #33
1978   "Before My Heart Finds Out" #23
1978   "You're A Part of Me" (w/Kim Carnes) #36
1979   "Like A Sunday in Salem" #40

Richie Furay
with *Buffalo Springfield*
1967   "For What It's Worth" #7
1967   "Bluebird" #58
1967   "Rock 'n' Roll Woman" #44
1968   "Expecting to Fly" #98
1968   "On the Way Home" #82

Chart information taken from Joel Whitburn's Record Research, compiled from Billboard's "Pop" charts.

with *Poco*
1970   "You Better Think Twice" #72
1971   "C'mon" #69

with *Souther, Hillman, Furay Band w/Al Perkins*
1974   "Fallin' in Love" #27

Chuck Girard
with the *Hondells*
1964   "Little Honda" #9
1964   "My Buddy Seat" #87
1966   "Younger Girl" #52

with the *Castells*
1961   "Sacred" #20
1961   "Make Believe Wedding" #98
1962   "So This Is Love" #21
1962   "Oh! What It Seemed To Be" #91

Edwin Hawkins Singers
1969   "Oh Happy Day" #4

Ray Hildebrand
with *Paul and Paula*
1962   "Hey Paula" #1
1963   "Young Lovers" #6
1963   "First Quarrel" #27
1963   "Something Old, Something New" #77
1963   "First Day Back at School" #60

McCrarys
1978   "You"

Barry McGuire
1965   "Eve of Destruction" #1
1966   "Child of Our Time" #72
1966   "Cloudy Summer Afternoon" #62

with the *New Christy Minstrels*
1962   "This Land Is Your Land" #93
1963   "Green, Green" #14
1963   "Saturday Night" #29
1964   "Today" #17
1964   "Silly Ol' Summertime" #92
1965   "Chim, Chim, Cheree" #81

Larry Norman
with *People*
1968   "I Love You" #14

Chart information taken from Joel Whitburn's Record Research, compiled from Billboard's "Pop" charts.

Michael Omartian
with the *Rhythm Heritage*
1975   "Theme from S.W.A.T." #1
1976   "Baretta's Theme (Keep Your Eye On the Sparrow)" #20
1977   "Theme from Rocky (Gonna Fly Now)" #94

Gary S. Paxton
with *Skip & Flip*
1959   "It Was I" #11
1959   "Fancy Nancy" #71
1960   "Cherry Pie" #11

with *Hollywood Argyles*
1960   "Alley Oop" #1

Dan Peek
with *America*
1972   "A Horse With No Name" #1
1972   "I Need You" #9
1972   "Ventura Highway" #8
1973   "Don't Cross the River" #35
1973   "Only In Your Heart" #62
1973   "Muskrat Love" #67
1974   "Tin Man" #4
1974   "Lonely People" #5
1975   "Sister Goldenhair" #1
1975   "Daisy Jane" #20
1975   "Woman Tonight" #44
1976   "Today's The Day" #23
1976   "Amber Cascades" #75

Billy Preston
1969   "That's the Way God Planned It" #62
1971   "My Sweet Lord" #90
1972   "That's the Way God Planned It" #65
1972   "Outa Space" #2
1972   "I Wrote A Simple Song" #77
1972   "Slaughter" #50
1973   "Will It Go Round in Circles" #1
1973   "Space Race" #4
1974   "You're So Unique" #48
1974   "Nothing From Nothing" #1
1974   "Struttin' " #22
1975   "Fancy Lady" #71

with the *Beatles*
1969   "Get Back" #1
1969   "Don't Let Me Down" #35

Cliff Richard
1959   "Living Doll" #30

Chart information taken from Joel Whitburn's Record Research, compiled from Billboard's "Pop" charts.

1963	"Lucky Lips" #62
1963	"It's All in the Game" #25
1964	"I'm the Lonely One" #92
1964	"Bachelor Boy" #99
1968	"Congratulations" #99
1976	"Devil Woman" #6
1976	"I Can't Ask for Anymore Than You" #80
1977	"Don't Turn the Light Out" #57

Turley Richards
1970	"Love Minus Zero—No Limit" #84
1970	"I Heard the Voice of Jesus" #99

Austin Roberts
1972	"Something's Wrong With Me" #12
1973	"Keep on Singing" #50
1975	"Rocky" #9

Nedra Ross
with *The Ronettes*
1963	"Be My Baby" #2
1963	"Baby, I Love You" #24
1964	"(The Best Part of) Breakin' Up" #39
1964	"Do I Love You" #34
1964	"Walking in the Rain" #23
1965	"Born to Be Together" #52
1965	"Is This What I Get for Loving You?" #75
1966	"I Can Hear Music" #100

Paul Stookey
1971	"Wedding Song (There Is Love)" #24

with *Peter, Paul & Mary*
1962	"Lemon Tree #35
1962	"If I Had A Hammer" #10
1962	"Big Boat" #93
1963	"Settle Down" #56
1963	"Puff the Magic Dragon" #2
1963	"Blowin' in the Wind" #2
1963	"Don't Think Twice, It's All Right" #9
1963	"Stewball" #35
1964	"Tell It on the Mountain" #33
1964	"Oh, Rock My Soul" #93
1965	"For Lovin' Me" #30
1965	"When the Ship Comes In" #91
1965	"Early Morning Rain" #91
1966	"The Cruel War" #52
1966	"The Other Side of This Life" #100
1967	"I Dig Rock and Roll Music" #9
1967	"Too Much of Nothing" #35
1969	"Day Is Done" #21
1969	"Leaving on a Jet Plane" #1

Chart information taken from Joel Whitburn's Record Research, compiled from Billboard's "Pop" charts.

B. J. Thomas

1966	"I'm So Lonesome I Could Cry" #8
1966	"Mama" #22
1966	"Billy and Sue" #34
1966	"Bring Back the Time" #75
1966	"Tomorrow Never Comes" #80
1967	"I Can't Help It (If I'm Still in Love with You)" #94
1968	"The Eyes of a New York Woman" #28
1968	"Hooked on a Feeling" #5
1969	"It's Only Love" #45
1969	"Pass the Apple, Eve" #97
1969	"Raindrops Keep Fallin' On My Head" #1
1970	"Everybody's Out of Town" #26
1970	"I Just Can't Help Believing" #9
1970	"Most of All" #38
1971	"No Love At All" #16
1971	"Mighty Clouds of Joy" #34
1971	"Long Ago Tomorrow" #61
1972	"Rock and Roll Lullaby" #15
1972	"That's What Friends Are For" #74
1972	"Happier Than the Morning Sun" #100
1975	"(Hey, Wontcha Play) Another Somebody Done Somebody Wrong Song" #1
1975	"Help Me Make It (To My Rockin' Chair)" #64
1977	"Don't Worry Baby" #17
1977	"Still the Loving Is Fun" #77
1978	"Everybody Loves a Rain Song"

Chart information taken from Joel Whitburn's Record Research compiled from Billboard's "Pop" charts.

Appendix C

A Complete Listing of All Known Jesus Music Recording Artists
and the Labels on Which They Have Recorded

It is often difficult to determine where to draw lines in describing different types
of contemporary Christian music. Is Christian folk music always Jesus music? Are
praise and scripture music considered contemporary gospel or Jesus music? As can
be seen on the charts in Appendix D, the distinctions are not easily made by any
means.

Thus, in an effort to make the list as comprehensive as possible, artists have each
been classified by the type of music they most often play or record.

For your aid in deciphering, here is a list of musical categories which have been
employed:

TYPES
cg—Contemporary Gospel
cl—Classical
cm—Catholic Music
co—Comedy
fm—Folk Music
jm—Jesus Music
jz—Jazz
ps—Praise/Scripture
rm—Rock Music (Secular-oriented)
sg—Soul Gospel
sr—Secular Release

COUNTRIES of ORIGIN
au—Australia
cn—Canada
it—Italy
sw—Sweden
uk—Great Britain

SPECIAL CODES
Ca—Cassette only on some releases
8T—8-track tape only on some releases
( )—When there are two groups with same
name, state or country of origin is given
in parenthesis.

Types of music performed by each artist or group are indicated by the first series
of letters. In many cases, combinations of code letters are used to identify the
artists' styles as specifically as possible. E.g., cg/jm/sg would indicate an artist
(such as Andraé Crouch) who performed or performs music which would appeal to
contemporary gospel, Jesus music, and soul gospel audiences.

In cases where the artists' records have originated or still originate from another
country, such country is shown by the letters in parentheses. (E.g., jm/uk would
indicate a Jesus music artist from Great Britain. Some or all of these artists' albums
may be available only in the country of origin.)

When "sr" is used, it means some or all albums by that artist or group have been
released by secular record companies only. Whether such artists are Christian or
not is not included in the codes.

Contemporary music of the Catholic church and Jesus music such as that
discussed in this book have generally appealed to different audiences. On the
whole, Catholic contemporary music has not permeated the non-Catholic scene to
any great degree. Therefore, Catholic contemporary music, of which the majority
is of a folk nature, is indicated by the letters "cm," with a further indication given
of specific style.

Without compiling an entire volume of listings, it is impossible to pinpoint the
exact types of music on recordings by the artists listed. Therefore, the codes given

should be considered guidelines only. Also, the listing is all-inclusive for Jesus music only. Artists representing other, sometimes closely related types of music are included, but the list of such artists is by no means complete.

Recordings of religious cults, or those recordings and artists deemed by the author more anti-Christian than Christian (such as "Jesus Christ Superstar") are not included. Quality of the recordings represented ranges from excellent to poor. Inclusion of any recording or artist on this list does not represent endorsement of the particular recording or artist, nor indicate the quality of the recordings. Many of the albums referred to are no longer available or carried by the actual labels; thus, they will take some scavenging to find.

This listing would hardly have been possible without the untiring help of Dan Hickling, editor and publisher of *Foreversong Journal*. Dan applied hours and hours of research into the compilation of this list. It should prove invaluable to anyone choosing to collect, broadcast or merchandise Jesus music.

CG	"Action Scene '71" (sampler)—Impact	CG	Amigos—Heart to Heart
CG/CO	Act One Company— Greentree	CG/JM	Amplified Version— NewPax, Chrism
CG	Acts—custom	CG	Andrus, Sherman— Impact, Shalom
CG	Adams, J. T. & the Fireside Singers—Word	CG	Andrus, Blackwood & Company—Greentree
JM	Adams, Randy—Star Song	SR/JM/CN	Apocalypse—Generation
JM/UK	Advocates—Dovetail	JM/CG	Archers—Charisma, Impact, Light
JM	Agape—Mark	CG	Arhelger, Jerry—Herald
CM/JM	Agape/St. Paul's School Choir—Mace	PS	"Arise and Shine" (various)— Scripture in Song
PS	Agape Force—Candle Co., Word	JM	Ark—Spirit
CM/FM	"A Hundred Fold" (sampler)— World Library	CG/JM	Armegeddon Experience—M/M
8T/JM	Airborne—Solid Rock Sound	JM/SG	Artistic Sounds—Savoy
CM/JM	A Joyful Noise— Ignatius House	JM	Aslan—Airborn
JM	Albrecht & Roley—Airborn	JM/CG	"A Time and A Place" (sampler)—Creative Sound
JM	Albrecht, Roley & Moore— White Horse	JM/UK	Atwood, Bill—Dovetail
JM/UK	Alethians—Myrrh	CG/JM	Autry, Tom—Star Song
JM	Alexandersen, Stephen— White Horse	JM	Ayala, Bob—Pure Joy, Myrrh
SR/SG	Allen Group, Rance—Gospel Truth, Truth, Capitol	CM/FM	Backwood—Pretzel
		CG	Bailey, Stan—Klesis
SR/JZ	All-Occasion Brass Band—MCA	JM	"Because I Am" (soundtrack)— Clear Light
JM	All-Saved Freak Band— Rock the World	JM/CG	"Beginnings" (sampler)— Sonrise Mercantile
CG	Alpenglow—JoySong, House Top	CG/FM	Believers—Doxa
		CM/JZ	Bellson Trio, Howard— World Library
JM	Altman, Terry Ross—Paraklete	CM/FM	Berakah—custom
CG	Amason Twins—Herald	CM/JM/IT	Berets—Blue Bell,

Avant Garde
SR/RM Berkery, Pat w/ Spur—
Glascow
JM/CG "Best of Christian Grit"
(sampler)—NewPax
JM Bethlehem—Maranatha
CG Blackwood, Debi—Clarion
JM/FM Blease, Jack—Prince of Peace
JM Blessitt, Arthur & Eternal Rush—
Creative Sound
CM/FM Blue, Robert—FEL
CM/FM Blunt, Neil &
C.P. Mudd—NALR
JM Boone Girls (The Boones)—
Lamb & Lion, Word
CG/JM Boone, Pat—Lamb & Lion
CG Boosahda, Stephanie—
Celebration, House Top
SR/JZ Branch, Ben and the Operation
Breadbasket Orch. & Chorus—
Checker
CG/JM Bridge—custom, Sword
JM Briggs, Tim—Superior
CG/UK Brightwinter—Myrrh
JM Brooks—Light
JM(CA) Brother Love—BeeGee
CG/CN Brotherlove—custom
JM Brothers w/Marj Snyder—
Discovery
JM/FM Brothers and Sisters—Agape
SG Brown, Phil & God's Earth
with Love—Rejoice
JM Brown, Scott Wesley—
Georgetown, NewPax, Sparrow,
Seven Locks
SR/JZ Brubeck, Dave—
Decca, Atlantic
JM/FM Bullock, Verne—Uriah (Ca)
CG Burton, Eddie—3rd Day
JM Burton, Wendell—Lamb & Lion
JM Butler, Dj—custom

SR/SG Caesar, Shirley—Hob,
Roadshow
JM Calfee, Pat—Morning Star
SR/SG California Earthquake—
United Artists
JM Camp, Steve—Myrrh
JM/AU Campbell, Peter—Trinity
JM Campi, Sandy—Lamb & Lion
JM/UK Canaan—Dovetail, Myrrh
SR/JM Canadian Rock Theatre—

Lion
PS Candle—Birdwing
JM/CG Carlson, Pete—custom,
Tempo, Chrism
JM/CG Carmichael, Carol
(Kim)—Light
CG Carmichael, Ralph—
Light, Sacred
CG "The Carpenter"
(musical)—Impact
JM/FM Case, Ron & Phil
Butin—custom
SR/JM/SG Caston & Majors—Motown
CG/JM/CN Centurions—Praise
JM Cephas—custom
CG Certain Sounds—Tempo
CG Changes—Herald
CG Channels—custom
CG Chapman, Dave—Milk
& Honey, Pilgrim
CG Chariot—Superior
JM Charisma—custom
CG Charity—Shalom
JM Chewning, Lawrence & Eastland
Band—Neoteric
CG/JM Children of the Day—
Maranatha, Light
JM Children of Faith—custom
CG Children of Light—
Milk & Honey
JM Children of the Light—
Sparrow
CG/SW Choralerna—Signatur, Myrrh,
Key, Sparrow
CG Chords—New Day
JM Christian, Chris—Myrrh
JM/CG "Christian People" (sampler)—
Lamb & Lion
JM/FM Chuck, Mary, & Friends
—Prince of Peace
JM Clark, Paul—Redeemer,
Creative Sound, Sonrise
Mercantile, Seed, Myrrh
JM Clark, Terry—Good News
CG Clawson, Cynthia—Triangle
JM Clockwise—Mans Hill
PS/UK Clouds—Dovetail
JM Cochran, Judy—custom
SR/JM/CN Cockburn, Bruce—True
North, Island
SR/SG Cogics—VJ International
SR/JM Colter, Jessi—Capitol

CM/FM	Comeau, Bill—Avant Garde
CG	"Come Together" (musical)—Light
CM/FM	"Come Winter, Come Lord" (sampler)—NALR
CG	Common Bond—Hope
CG	Common Ground—Tempo
PS	"Communion" (various)—Birdwing
JM	Concrete Rubber Band—American Artists custom
CM/FM	Condon, Tom—World Library
CG	Continentals—Light, Word
CG	Cook, Cheri—Solid Rock Sound
JM/UK	Cook, David—EMI
CF/CN	Cooney, Sr. Lorna—Unicom, Praise
JM	Copalello, Pat—Kerygma
CG/UK	Cordner, Rodney—Dorian, Pilgrim
CG	Coryell, Randy—Image VII
JM	Cotton, Gene—Monya, Impact, Myrrh
CG(CA)	Crain, Jim—Star Song
CM/FM	Creed, Dan—NALR
JM	Crimson Bridge—Myrrh
CG	"Cross & The Switchblade" (soundtrack)—Light
CG	Cross Current Community—Avant Garde
JM/CG/SG	Crouch, Andrae & the Disciples—Light
SR/JM	Crusaders—Capitol
CG	Cruse Family—Canaan
JM	"Cry 3" (soundtrack)—Clear Light
CG/JM	Cull, Bob—Armchair, Maranatha
CM/FM	Cullen, Pat II—Joral
CG	Culverwell, Andrew—Polydor, DaySpring (*UK*)
CG	Curry, Marie—Herald
CM/FM	Curzio, Elaine—Avant Garde
CG	Dalton, Larry—Light
JM	Dalton, Michael—Sounds of Joy
JM	Damascus—Eden
JM	Damascus Road—JesuSongs

CM/FM	Dameans—FEL, TeleKetics, NALR
SR/JZ/CN	Dandy, Trevor—Zaza
JM	Daniel Amos—Maranatha
CG	Danny, Wayne, Paul—Image VII
CG	Daubenton, Georgene—Edify
JM/UK	Davies, Graham—Sharing
SR/JZ	Davis, Rev. Gary—Folklore, Prestige
JM	"Dawntreader One" (sampler)—Star Song
JM	Daybreak—Holy Kiss
CG	Daylight—Edify
CG	Dayspring—Word
SR/JM	Deasy, Mike—Capitol
JM	Deasy, Mike & Kathie—Sparrow
JM	DeGarmo & Key—Lamb & Lion
JM/CG/SG	DeGrate, Don & the Delegation—Sword, Shalom
CG/JM	Deliverance—Image VII, NewPax
JM	Denzien, Rick—Superior
CG	Devers, Marcy—Olde Towne
SG	Dickerson, Ron & the Tranquillity—New Day
CM/FM	Diesel, Paula—Avant Garde
SG	Dixon, Jessy—Light
JM	Dogwood—Lamb & Lion, Myrrh
JM	Dove—Myrrh, Shalom
JM	Drake, Ed—Holy Kiss
CM/JM	Dumin, Frank—Avant Garde
CG	Duncan, D. J. W/Tim Goble—Destiny
JM	Dust—Myrrh
JM/FM	Dust & Ashes—Avant Garde
JM	East of the Altar—custom
JM	"Easy Said . . ." (musical)—CMP
CG	"Edify Volume 1" (sampler)—Edify
CM/FM	Edwards, Deanna—TeleKetics, NALR
CM/JM	Edwin, Robert—Avant Garde, Fortress
JM	Eldridge, Rick—Herald, Klesis
SR/RM	Electric Prunes—Reprise
CM/JZ	Elia, Tim—NALR
SR/JZ	Ellington, Duke—Prestige, RCA

JM/FM	Ellis & Lynch—Raven, Ra-O
JM	Emmanuel—Chalice
CG	Epstein, Kathie—Petra
JM	Eternal Savings and Trust
	Company—Amphion
JM	Eternity Express—
	Skylight Sing
JM	Exkursions—custom
CG	Expressions—JoySong
CM/FM	Fabing, Bob—NALR
JM/FM	Family—Mannafest
CM/FM	"Family Album" (sampler)—
	Epoch Universal
JM/AU	Family (Tree)—M7,
	Lamb & Lion
JM	Farrell & Farrell—NewPax
JM/PS	"Father's Family Album"
	(various)—Temple Tone
CG	Feist, Lydell—Edify,
	Golden Streets
JM	Field, Fred—Maranatha
JM	"Firewind" (musical)—
	Sparrow
JM	Fireworks—Myrrh
JM	First Gear—Myrrh
JM	Fischer, John—FEL, Light
JM/UK	Fish Company—Myrrh,
	Grapevine
PS	Fisherfolk—Net, Celebration
JM	Fishermen—Great Awakening
CF/PS	Foley, John—NALR
CM/FM	Foley & Kavanaugh—custom
CM/FM	Followers of the
	Way—custom
JM	Ford, Delvin—Light
JM/FM	Forerunners—Creative Sound
CG	"Forever Promised"
	(musical)—custom
CG/JM	Found Free—Olde Towne,
	Greentree
SR/RM	Fowler, Bubba—Columbia
CG/JM	Francisco, Don—NewPax
CG	Frangipane, Francis—Beracah
CM/SG	"Freeing the Spirit"
	(various)—custom
CA	Friendly People—custom
JM/CN	Friends of Jesus—custom
SR/RM	Furay Band, Richie—Asylum
CG/FM	Gamble Folk—Creative
	Sound, Edify
CG	Gardner, Reba Rambo—

	Impact, Greentree
JM	Garrett, Glenn—
	custom, Jesus Folk
CM/FM	Garza, Juliana—NALR
CG	Gassman, Clark—Light
JM	Gentle Faith—Maranatha
CG	Gilbert, Jim—Light
JM	Gill, Jim—Star Song
JM	Girard, Chuck—Good News
JM	Glad—Myrrh
SR/JM	Glass Harp—Decca, Star Song
JM	Glory Bound—custom
JM	Glory Road—Hand in Hand
SR	"Godspell" (soundtrack)—
	Bell, Arista
SR/JM	God Squad—Rare Earth
JM	Goins, Doug—Discovery
CG/JM	"Good Jesus Music Inside"
	(various)—Superior
CG	"Good News" (musical)—
	Broadman
SR/UK	Good News—Columbia, CBS
JM(CA)	Good News—Maranatha,
	Sonrise Mercantile
CG	Good News Circle—
	Sonrise Mercantile, Light
JM(VT)	Good News
	Messengers-House
JZ	Good News Singers—custom
CG/CN	Gospel Peace—Praise
JM	Gospel Seed—Myrrh
JM	"Gospel Ship"
	(sampler)—Destiny
JM	"Gospel Ship II"
	(sampler)—Destiny
CG/CN	Gossetts—Praise
JM/UK	Gould, Kevin—Key,
	Myrrh, Grapevine
CG/JM	Grandquist, Nancy—
	Freedom, NewPax
JM	Grant, Amy—Myrrh
CG	Great Commission Company—
	M/M, custom
JM	Great Jubilation—Rainbow
JM	"Greatest of These Is Love"
	(sampler)—Myrrh
JM	"Great Great Joy"
	(sampler)—Myrrh
SR/SG	Green, Al—Hi
JM	Green, Keith—Sparrow
JM/CG	Green, Lilly—Destiny, Myrrh
JM	Green, Tom & Candy—
	Superior, Green Mountain

JM	Green, Tom & Sherry—Big Rock
SR/JM/CG	Greene, Jeannie—Elektra
JM/CG	"Greentree Sampler Album" (sampler)—Greentree
JM/FM	Greenway, Blake—Century One
CM/FM	Griffen, Ron & the Leaven—FEL
CG/JM	Grine, Janny—Sparrow
CM/FM	Group—World Library
CG/JM/SG	Grover, Teddy & Joy—custom, Greentree
CM/FM/JM	Gutfruend, Ed—Epoch VII, NALR
CM/FM	Habjan, Sr. Germaine—FEL
CG/CN	Hakumu—Christopher
SG	Haley, Josh—Songbird
JM/SG	Hall, Danniebelle—Light, Sparrow
CG	Hall, Duann—custom
JM	Hall, Pam Mark—Aslan, Spirit
CG/JM	Hall, Sammy—Faith, Impact, NewPax, Pax
JM	Hallelujah Joy Band—Creative Sound
CM/RM	Haney, Lynn—Tribute
JM	Haney, Marc—Bride
CG	Harlan, John, Todd—Disciple
CG	Harris, Larnelle—Word
JM/FM(NM)	Harvest—Gospel Towne (FM)
JM(CA)	Harvest—Pure Joy
JM	Harvest Flight—Destiny
JM/FM	Haun, Mike & Jerry Blacklaw—custom
SR/SG	Hawkins, Edwin—Pavillion, Buddha, Birthright
SG	Hawkins, Tramaine—Light
SG	Hawkins, Walter—Light
SR/UK	Haworth, Bryn—Island, A&M
JM/UK	Hayles, Lou—Myrrh
JM	Heard, Mark—AB, Airborn
JM	Henderson, Ken—Straight
JM/UK	Henderson, Stewart—Dovetail
CG	Henley, Bob & Jane—Singcord
CG	"Here Comes the Son" (musical)—Light
CG	Heritage—Medallion
JM	Annie Herring—Sparrow
FM	Hershberg, Sarah—FEL
SR/JM	Hester, Benny—VMI, Spirit
JM/UK	Hewitt, Garth—Myrrh
CG/JM	Hibbard, Bruce—Seed, Myrrh
CG/JM	Hildebrand, Ray—Word, Myrrh, Tempo
JM	"Hill Country Faith Festival '74" (sampler)—custom
SG	Hill, Tessie—Peacock
CM/FM	His People—World Library
CG	Holm, Dallas (& Praise)—New Sounds, Impact, Greentree
JM	Honeytree, Nancy—Superior, Myrrh
JM	Hoopes, Dick—Celebration
SR/JM	Hope—A&M
JM	Hope of Glory—Shalom, Tempo, Chrism
JM	Hopkins, Dave—custom
JM/FM	Horn & Alexander—Bridge
CG/UK	"Hosanna" (musical)—Reflection
JM	Howard, Tom—Solid Rock
JM	Howell, Doug—Trinity, Eden
CG	Hubbell, Larry—Myrrh
CM/FM	Hurd, Bob & Whitebird—FEL
JM	Hurlburt, Steve—Last Adam
CG	Hutton, Ramona—Impact
JM	Hybl, Scott—Ark
CG	Icthus Team—Destiny
CG/PS	"If My People" (musical)—Light
JM	Imago Dei—Caelix
CG	"I'm Here, God's Here, Now We Can Start" (musical)—Light
CG	Imperials—Impact, DaySpring
CG	"In the Spirit" (sampler)—Bridge
CO	Isaac Air Freight—Maranatha
JM/UK	Ishmael—Dovetail
CG	"It's Getting Late" (musical)—Light
CM/FM	Jabusch, Willard F.—One O One
JM/FM	Jackson Brothers—custom
SG	Jackson Company, Henry—Myrrh, Gospel Truth, Birthright
SG	Jackson, Madeline Manning-NewPax
SR/RM	James, Tommy—Roulette
JM	J.C. & Co.—custom
JM	Power Outlet—Myrrh
CG/CO	Jeremiah People—

Continental, Light

JM "Jesus Festival of Music"
(sampler) Creative Sound

JM "Jesus Folk One"
(sampler)—Jesus Folk

JM "Jesus Loves You"
(various)—Hosanna

JM "Jesus People" (sampler)
—Creative Sound

JM "Jesus Power" (sampler)
—Creative Sound

JM/CG "Jesus Sound Explosion"
(various)—custom

JM/UK John, Alexander—Myrrh

JM/CG John & Kathy, Shane &
Alice—NewPax

CG Johnson, Bob & Maxine
—Herald

JM Johnson, Jeff—Ark

JM Johnson, Karen—
Freedom Light

CG Johnson, Kathie Lee—
Petra

JM Johnson, Mike—custom,
Creative Sound, Freedom Light,
JoySong, NewPax, CAM

CG Johnson, Paul—Bridge,
Chapel, Light, Petra

JM/FM Jonathan & Charles—
Inter-Varsity

CF Joncas, Mike—World Library

JM Joshua—Impact

PS "Joy Album" (various)—
Maranatha

JM(IL) Joyful Noise—custom

JM(IA) Joyful Noise—custom

JM/FM Joyful Revolution—
World Library

CG/JM Joyous Celebration—Listen

JM/UK Joy Strings—Regal
Zonophone, Epic

CG "Jubilation" (musical)—Impact

JM "Jubilation!" (sampler)—Myrrh

JM "Jubilation, Too!"
(sampler)—Myrrh

JM/FM Kanewske, Kathy—Mayim

CG Kathie & Michie—Petra

JM Keaggy, Phil—New Song,
Star Song

JM Kelly, Judy—New Life

JM/UK Kendrick, Graham—Impact,
Key, Dovetail

JM/CG Kentucky Faith—Mark

CG Kerner, Debby—Maranatha

JM/UK "The Key Collection"
(sampler)—Key

PS Keyhole—Net, GIA

JM/FM Kinfolk—custom

CG King, George & the Fellow-
ship—Tempo, Olde Towne
King's Children—King's
Center

JM Klesis—Herald

JM Knights of the Lord's Table
—Holy Kiss

SR/CM/FM Kowalewski, Paul—Public
Affair

JM Krauss, Bill—Chara

CM/FM Krikston, Daniel—World
Library

JM Lafferty, Karen—Maranatha

JM Lamb—Messianic

CG Lambert, Kyle—Rose, Sonrise Mercantile

CM/FM/PS Landry, Carey—custom,
NALR

JM/FM Last Day—New Life

JM/FM Last Days—custom

CG Latinos—Lamb & Lion,
custom

JM/CG Lee, Danny & the Children
of Truth—RCA, Impact

JM LeFevra, Ray— Holy Kiss

SR/JM LeFevre, Mylon—Cotillion

CG Lentz, Roger—custom

CG Lewis, Erv—Impact,
Herald

PS Liberated Wailing Wall—
Hineni, Tempo

JM/UK Liberation Suite—Myrrh

CG/CN Light—Mello D

JM/UK Lightbearers—Dovetail

PS Lighthouse—Word of God

JM Limpic & Rayburn—Fanfare,
Myrrh

PS Lion of Judah—custom

JM/UK "Live at Spre-e Album"
(various)—Key

JM/UK The Lively Ones—Word (CG)

CM/FM Living Spirit—NALR

JM/UK "Lonesome Stone" (musical)
—Reflection

CG Long, Candi—custom

CM/FM Louvat, Lorraine—custom,

	Fiat, Joral
CG	"Love" (musical)—Tempo
JM/PS	Love Inn Company—New Song
JM	"Love, Peace, Joy" (sampler)—Myrrh
JM	Love Song—Good News
CG	Love Song Strings—Creative Sound, Mighty Wind
CG	Lovette, Carol Jean—Celebration
CG	Lowe, Candi—custom
CG/JM	Lucas, Sharalee—Word, Petra, Greentree
JM/UK	MacKenzie, Judy—Impact, EMI
CG/UK	Magee, Len—Impact, Dovetail, Grapevine
JM/UK	Malcolm & Alwyn—Myrrh, Pye, Key
JM	Malool, Greg—Herald
CG/JM	Manley, Jim—New Wine
CG	Mann Singers, Johnny—Light
JM(PA)	Manna—Manna
JM(FL)	Manna—Herald
JM	"Maranatha! 1—The Everlasting Living Jesus Music Concert" (various)—Maranatha
JM	"Maranatha! 2" (various)—Maranatha
JM	"Maranatha! 3—Rejoice in the Lord" (various)—Maranatha
JM	"Maranatha! 4" (various)—Maranatha
JM	"Maranatha! 5" (various)—Maranatha
JM	"Maranatha! 6—A Family Portrait" (various)—Maranatha
PS/CG	Maranatha Singers—Maranatha
PS/CG	Maranatha Strings—Maranatha
JM	Mark, Pam—Aslan
JM/CN	Marnoch, Ray—custom (FM)
CG	Marsh, Don (Brass Orchestra)—Impact
JM	Martin, Rich—Sonburst
CG/CN	Martin, Sara Dale—Profile

SR/CL/RM	"Mass" (opera)—Columbia
JM	Matthews, Randy—Word, Myrrh
JM	Matthews, Taylor & Johnson—NewPax
JM	Mattson, Dave—Myrrh
JM	McCrary—Light
SR/FM	McCurdy, Ed—Folkways
JM	McGee, Barry—Sword
JM	McGuire—Greentree
JM	McGuire, Barry—Myrrh, Sparrow
JM	McHugh, Phill—Triad, Jesus Folk, Lamb & Lion
CG/UK	McKee, Mary—Pilgrim
JM	McPheeters, Charles—Landmark
JM	McVay, Lewis—Maranatha
CG	Medema, Ken—Word
CM/FM	Medical Mission Sisters—Avant Garde
JM	Meece, David—Myrrh
CG	"Meet God, Man" (opera)—Concordia
JM/UK	"Meet Jesus Music"—Profile, Dovetail
JM	Melton, Carol—Agape
JM	Messenger—Light
CG	Messengers of Love—custom
CG	Michael & Tamara—Birthright, New Life
CM/FM	Miffleton, Jack—World Library
SR/SG	Mighty Clouds of Joy—ABC Dunhill
JM/UK	Mighty Flyers—Myrrh, Trust
JM	Millenium—custom
CG	Miller, Jimmy—Pure Joy, DaySpring
CG	Mills, Walt—Impact, Myrrh, DaySpring
SR/JM	Mind Garage—RCA
SR/CM/RM	Mission—Tribute, Avant Garde, Paramount
CM/RM	Mitchell, Ian & Caroline—FEL
JM	"Moment of Truth" (various)—custom, Sonrise Mercantile
SR/CG/JM	Monda, Dick—Verve
CM/JZ	Montague Trio,

	George—FEL	CG	New Sky Singers—
CM/FM	Montfort Mission—		Volume III
	Warner Brothers, GIA	PS	New Song—New
SR/RM	Moonrakers—Shamley		Song Ministries
CM/CG	Moore, Alan—World Library	CG	"New Vibrations"
JM/FM	Moore, Mickey &		(musical)—Light
	Becki—Maiden	CG	New Village Singers—
JM/FM	Moore, Ron—Airborn,		Edify
	Creative Sound	JM	New Wine—Deep
CM/FM	Mudd, C.P.—Jonah	CG/FM	"New Wine Sound"
JM/CN	Murphy, Ray & Dana		(various)—New Wine
	Gillespie—Christopher	CG/FM	"New Wine 2"—
CG/UK	Murray, Gwen—Dovetail		New Wine
JM	Mustard Seed Faith—	CG	New World—FourMost
	Maranatha	JM	Norman, Larry—Capitol,
JM	"Mystery Revealed"		Impact, One Way, Verve,
	(sampler)		MGM, Solid Rock,
	—Creative Sound		AB, Street Level
		FM/JM/CN	North Wind—
			Master's Collection
JM/UK	Narnia—Myrrh	JM/UK	Nutshell—Myrrh
CG	"Natural High"		
	(musical)—Light		
CG	Nelson, Dan—Listen	CG	Oak Ridge Boys—
JM	Nelson, Erick—Maranatha		Columbia
CM/FM	Nestor, Leo—	CG/JM	Oaks Band—
	World Library		Rockland Road
JM	New Beginning—custom	JM	O'Connell, James—
CG/JM	Newbury Park—		Sonburst
	Creative Sound	JM	Omartian, Michael (& Stormie)
CG	New Californians—		—ABC Dunhill, Myrrh
	Tempo	JM	One Song—Paula
CM/FM	New Canticle—	JM	One Truth—Sonrise
	Word of God		Mercantile, Greentree
CG	"New Covenant"	PS	ORU Vespers—Celebration
	(musical)—Light	SR/JM	Overland Stage—Epic
JM	New Covenant/Grace—	JM	Owens (-Collins),
	Dayspring House		Jamie—Light
CG	New Creation—custom	CG	Owens, Jimmy—Word,
CG	New Creation—Heritage		Light, Impact
CG/PS	New Creation Singers—	JM	Owens, Jon—Gospel Now
	Family Crusades, Birdwing		Sound, Psalms &
CG	New Dawn—Greentree		Proverbs, Windy
CG	New Directions—Herald		
CG	New Folk—Impact	CM/FM	Page, Paul F.—Pretzel
CG	New Folk—custom	JM/FM	Pampayan, Ted—
CG	New Hope (Singers)—		Silent Seed
	Light, Tempo	JM	Pantano/Salsbury—
CG/UK	New Horizon—Pilgrim		Solid Rock
CG/JM	New Jerusalem—Trinity	JM/UK	Pantry, John—
JM	New Life—Trinity		Maranatha
CG	New Neighborhood—	JM	Parable—Maranatha
	Creative Sound	JM/UK	Parchment—Pye,

	Myrrh, Grapevine
CM/FM	Parker, Tom— World Library
CM/FM	Patenaude, Andre— Shrine
JM	Pattons—Candle Co.
CG/JM	Paxton, Gary S.— NewPax, Pax
JM(CA)	Peculiar People—custom
JM	Peek, Dan— Lamb & Lion
CG/FM	"People Got to Be Free" (various)—FourMost
PS	People of Praise— custom
CG/CN	Pepper, Pat— Master's Collection
JZ	Person, Houston—Savoy
CG	Petersen, Dave—Freedom
JM	Petra—Myrrh
JM	Phoenix Sonshine— Destiny, Maranatha
JM	Pilgrim 20—CHM
FM	Pires, Barbara—custom
CG/CN	Pollard, Elaine—Praise
CG/UK	Pope, Dave—Myrrh
JM/UK	Potter, Phil—Genesis
CG/CN	Potter's Clay—Today
JM	Powell, Steve—Wineskin
CG/CN	Power & Light Co.—Today
JM	"Power Music" (sampler)— Myrrh
JM	Praise—Creative Sound, custom
CF/JZ/JM	"Praise the Lord in Many Voices, Volumes I–III"—Avant Garde
SG	Preston, Billy—Myrrh
FM	Pritcher, Joan—custom
JM	Psalm 150—Manna
JM/FM	Quinlan, Paul— FEL, NALR
JM/CN	Quintessance— Christopher
JM	Rainbow Promise— Wine Press
CG	Rambo, Reba—Impact
CG	Random Sample—Tempo
CG	Raney, Sue—Light
CG	"Real Thing, The" (various)—Word

FM/JM/UK	Reality Folk—Profile
JM/FM	Rebirth—Avant Garde, custom
JM/CN	Reborn—custom
JM(NJ)	Redemption—Triumphonic
JM(TX)	Redemption—Evan Comm
CG	Reflection—Word
CG	"Relevant" (sampler)— Bridge
JM	Remnant—custom
CG	Renewal—Rockland Road
CM/FM	Repp, Ray—FEL, Myrrh, Agape, Joral
CG	"Requiem for a Nobody" (various)—Light
JM/CN	Restoration—Praise
JM/CA	Resurrection Band— custom, Star Song
JM/CG	Rettino, Ernie— Maranatha, Windchime
SG/CN	Revelation Company— Master's Collection
JM/UK	Reynard—Grapevine
FM	Rich, Linda— Inter-Varsity
CG/JM/UK	Richard, Cliff— Columbia, Word, Light, EMI
JM/FM	Ridings, Rick—Selah
JM	Rising Hope—custom
CM/FM	Roamin' Brothers—FEL
CM/FM	Roamin' Collars— World Library
CG	Robbins, Terri—custom
JM	Roberts, Austin & Advent—NewPax
JM/SG	Robinson, Eddie—Myrrh
JM	Rockwood—Dharma
CG	Romero, Judy— Lamb & Lion
JM	Ron & Shirley w/ Universe—custom
JM	Ross, Nedra—New Song
CM/FM	Rousseau, Robert—FEL
JM	Ryder, Dennis—Hosanna
CM/FM	St. Louis Jesuits—NALR
JM	Salmondt & Mulder—custom
FM/JM/CN	Salte, Arlen—Eagle Creek
JM	Salvation Air Force—Myrrh
CM/FM	Sanders, Skipp— World Library
PS/CA	Sandquist, Ted—

	New Song
CM/FM	Sarkissian, Kevin & Clare—custom
FM	Scannell, Jim—People's Music
CG	Schell Company, Jack—Dawn
SR/CL/RM	Schifrin, Lalo—Verve
CM/FM	Schoembachler, Tim—NALR
CM/FM	Scholtes, Peter—FEL
FM/UK	Scott, Dana & the Crown Folk—BBC
PS	"Scripture Songs" (various)—Hosanna
SR/RM	Seawind—CTI, Horizon
FM	Sebastian, Nancy—custom
JM	Second Chapter of Acts—Myrrh, Sparrow
JM	Seeds—Jubilation, Klesis
JM	Selah—Singcord, Milk & Honey
CM/FM	Servants of the Light—custom
JM/CG	Session, Glynna—Chrism
JM	Seth—Shalom
CG/CN	Shalom—Christopher
CG/CN	Shalom—Praise
CG/UK	Sharon People—Sharing
CG	Sharretts—Word, DaySpring
CM/FM	Shaw, Jim—FEL
JM/UK	Sheep, The—Myrrh
CG/JM/CN	Shepherd's Flock—Christopher, Master's Collection, Praise
JM	Sheppard, Tim—Greentree
JM(CA)	Shiloh—Adriel, Sonburst, Lamb & Lion
CG(NY)	Shiloh—custom
JM(TX)	Shiloh—CMP
CG	"Show Me" (musical)—Impact
JM	Signs of the Time—CMP
JM/CN	Simeon—Master's Collection
JM	Simple Truth—Creative Sound, Tempo
CG	Sinclair, Jerry—CAM
JM	Sipple, Barbara—Lazarus
CG ·	Sixth Day—Light
CG	Skillings Singers, Otis—Tempo
FM	Smith, Eddie—Tempo
CG	Smith, Moose—House Top
CG	Smith, Paul—Eagle Wing
JM/CG/Ca	Smith, Tom—custom
JM/UK	Snell, Adrian—Dovetail, Maranatha
JM	Snyder, Marj—Discovery
CM/FM	"SOAR Folk Hymnal" (various)—FEL
CG	Song of Deliverance—Tempo
PS/UK	"Songs of Worship and Praise" (various)—Word
JM	Sonlight—Light
CG/JM	SonLight Orchestra—Myrrh
CG/JM	Sonshine Circle—Light
CG/JM	Sonship—Olde Towne, Messianic
JM	Sons of Thunder—Bronte
JM/UK	"Sonsong" (musical)—Zebra
JM	Sons Unto Glory—custom
JM	"The Son Worshipers" (soundtrack)—One Way
SG/JM	Soul Liberation—Creative Arts
CG/CN	Soul Survivors—Mello D, Master's Collection
JM	Sound Foundation—Mark
CG/UK	Sound Purpose—Word
CG	Sounds of Celebration—Light
JM	Sounds of Joy—Shalom, JoySong
FM/JM/CN	Sounds of Light—Mansion
CG	"Sounds of the 'Now' Generation" (sampler)—Word
CG	Sounds of the Spirit—custom
SR/CM/FM	Sourire, Sr.—Philips
JM	"Sparrow Spotlight Sampler"—Sparrow
CG	Spectrums, The—Creative Sound
CG	Spirit of Love—Word
JM	Spoelstra, Mark—Aslan
SR/RM	Spooky Tooth—A&M

JM	Spradlin, Byron—Light
CG/CN	"Spread the News" (sampler)—Today
JM	Spring of Joy— Lamb & Lion
CG/JM	Springwater—Springwater
CG	Spurrlows—Word, Light, Tempo
JM	Stanley, Carl—Light
SR/SG	Staple Singers—Stax
JM	Stearman, Dave— Celebration
SR/CG	Stevens, Ray—Barnaby
JM	Stewart & Kyle— Grapevine, Chrism
JM	Stonehill, Randy— Solid Rock, One Way
JM	Stookey, Noel Paul— Warner Brothers, Neworld
JM	Strathdee, Jim—New Wine
SR/JM	Street Christians—PIP
JM	Sugar, Chuck—Jasper
CM/JZ	Summerlin, Ed— Avant Garde
SR/JM	Summers, Bob—MGM
JM	Suncast—Daybreak, Myrrh
JM	Sundquist, James— Lamb & Lion
JM	"Superjubilation!" (sampler)—Myrrh
JM	Suriano, Gregg—Behold
CG	Sutter, Lynn— DaySpring
JM	Sweet Comfort (Band)— Maranatha, Light
SR/RM	Sweet Revival—SSS
JM/CN	Sweet Spirit—Christopher
SG/JM(NY)	Sweet Spirit—Shalom
JM	Sycomore—Celebration
CM/FM	Sylvester, Erich— Epoch VII
CG	Take Three—Bridge
JM	Talbot Brothers—Warner Brothers, Sparrow
JM	Talbot, John Michael— Sparrow
JM	Talbot, Terry—Sparrow
JM	"Tales from the Tube" (Soundtrack)—Creative Sound
PS	Tamarah—custom
CG/JM	Tami Cheri—Light, Superior

SR/CL	Tashi—RCA Red Seal
JM	Taylor, Danny—Jubal, Tempo, NewPax
JM	Taylor, Emmett— Kerygma
JM	Taylor, Joe—Ark
CG	"Teen Challenge Praise" (various)
JM/CG	"Teen Scene" (various)— Charisma
CG	"Tell It Like It Is" (musical)—Light
CG	"Tell the World in '73" (musical)—Light
CM/FM	Temple, Sebastian— St. Francis
CM/FM	Temple/Hershberg— St. Francis
CM/FM	10.15—custom
JM	Terry Group, The Pat— Myrrh, custom
JM/SG	Thedford, Bili— Good News
CG/UK	The Genesis—Pilgrim
CG	Theisen, Maribeth— Celebration
JM	Third Day—custom
JM	Thomas, B.J.—Myrrh
CG	Thomas, Harry—Destiny
CG	Thomas, Tina—Superior
JM/FM	Tim & Dale—Ark
JM	"Time to Run" (soundtrack)— World Wide, Creative Sound
JM	Tom & Dan—FEL
CG/SW	Tornquist, Evie— Majestic, Signatur, Word
CG/JM	"To the Children of the King" (various)—Sheep Shed
SR/SG	Townsley, Jr., Nat— ABC Peacock
JM	Tranquility—Chrism
JM	Trinity—Living Waters
CG	Truth & His Associates— Truth
CG/JM	Truth—Impact, Paragon
JM	"Truth of Truths" (musical)—Oak
CM/FM	Tucciarone, Angel— World Library
JM	Ugartechea, Becky— Maranatha
JM	"Ultima Thule" (sampler)—

Creative Sound
CG Union, The—Elkanah
CG Unknown Quantity—Creative Sound
SR/RM U.S. Apple Corps—SSS
FM Uzilevsky, Marcus—Oaksprings

CG Vagle, Fred & Anna Mae—custom
JM Valley, Jim—Light
JM/CG Van Dyke, Vonda Kay—Word, Myrrh
CM/FM Vickers, Wendy—Epoch VII
SR/JM/JZ Vincent, James—Caribou
CG Vision—Light

FM Wake Up My People—custom
JM/UK Wall Band, Alwyn—Myrrh
JM Wall Brothers Band—Greentree
JM/CG Ward, James—Peniel, Dharma
CO Warnke, Mike—Myrrh
JM/UK Water Into Wine Band—Myrrh
JM Way, The—Maranatha
CG Wedgewood—Creative Sound, Bridge
CG/JM Whetstine, Don—custom
JM "Whisper His Name All Day Long" (various)—Destiny
JM/CG Whittemore, Dan—custom, Tempo, Chrism
JM/JZ Wiley, Fletch—Star Song
JM Willard, Kelly—Maranatha

CG/FM Williams, Dick—Hosanna
JM/FM Williams, Jon 'n' Rachel—custom
SR/JZ Williams, Mary Lou—Mary
JM/CN Williston, Bob—Praise
JM Wilson McKinley—Voice of Elijah
SR/FM Winslow, Tom—Biograph
CM/FM Wise, Joe—Fontaine House
CG "Witness, The" (musical)—Light
CO Witte, John & Viccijo—Shalom
JM Woods, Barry—Holy Kiss
CG Wootten, Bubba—Glory House
PS Word of God—Word of God

JM/CG/UK "Ye Olde London Bus Christian Bookshop & Boutique Souvenir Record" (sampler)—Dovetail
CG Yesterday, Today & Forever—Carman
JM Ylvisaker, John & Amanda—Avant Garde
JM/FM Yonker, John & David—custom, Edify
JM York, Randy—Rockwood
CG Young and Free—Word
CG Young Church Singers—Word

FM Zion Mountain Folk—Light
CM/FM Zsigray, Joe—NALR

Appendix D
GOSPEL MUSIC 1964 & 1979

As is very obvious by the charts on the following pages, there was very little truly contemporary music for Christians in 1964. There was *no* rock counterpart in the gospel realm, and folk music was allowed to infiltrate only through youth choruses or praise/scripture songs. (Praise/scripture songs were referred to in those days as gospel choruses.)

By 1979, every secular form of music short of punk rock had its counterpart in Christian music. Both contemporary gospel and Jesus music had added extensively to the variety of Christian music available.

Solid lines on the charts indicate a direct influence and dotted lines indicate an indirect or occasional influence.

Gospel Music—1964

Secular Parallels and/or Influences

Christian Music Styles

Spirituals

Country & Western

Southern Gospel

Rhythm & Blues

Appalachian Folk

Jazz

Soul Gospel

Rock

Folk

Praise/Scripture

Pop Ballads

Big Band

Children's Gospel

Easy-Listening

Traditional Gospel/Inspirational

Classical

Hymns

——— Direct Influence

– – – Direct Influence Indirect or Occasional Influence

Gospel Music—1979

Secular Parallels and/or Influences

Christian Music Styles

Direct Influence
Direct Influence
Indirect or Occasional Influence

Country & Western
Spirituals
Rhythm & Blues & Soul Music
Appalachian Folk
Jazz
Rock
Folk
Pop Ballads
Big Band
Easy-Listening
Classical

Jesus Music

Southern Gospel
Soul Gospel
Folk Musicals
Praise/Scripture
Contemporary Gospel
Children's Gospel
Traditional Gospel/Inspirational
Hymns

Appendix E
BIBLIOGRAPHY AND SUGGESTED READING

(Several of the books listed in the bibliography are now out of print. Copies may still be found in some Christian bookstores or church libraries. * Indicates a book especially recommended.)

The Jesus Movement
Beck, Hubert. *Why Can't the Church Be Like This?* St. Louis, Missouri: Concordia Publishing House, 1973.
*Benson, Dennis C. *The Now Generation.* Richmond, Virginia: John Knox Press, 1969.
Blessitt, Arthur. *Life's Greatest Trip.* Waco, Texas: Word Books, 1970.
Blessitt, Arthur; with Walter Wagner. *Turned on to Jesus.* New York: Hawthorne Books, Inc., 1971.
Blessitt, Arthur. *Tell the World: A Manual for Jesus People.* Old Tappan, New Jersey: Fleming H. Revell Company, 1972.
Briscoe, Stuart. *Where Was the Church When the Youth Exploded?* Grand Rapids: Zondervan Publishing House, 1972.
*Graham, Billy. *The Jesus Generation.* Grand Rapids: Zondervan Publishing House, 1971.
Lindsey, "Holy" Hubert. *Bless Your Dirty Heart.* Plainfield, New Jersey: Logos International, 1972.
Moody, Jess. *The Jesus Freaks.* Waco, Texas: Word Books, 1971.
Ortega, Reuben, compiler. *The Jesus People Speak Out!* Elgin, Illinois: David C. Cook Publishing Co., 1972.
Pederson, Duane; with Bob Owen. *Jesus People.* Glendale, California: Regal Books, 1971.
*Plowman, Edward E. *The Underground Church.* Elgin, Illinois: David C. Cook Publishing Co., 1971.
*Quebedeaux, Richard. *The Young Evangelicals.* New York: Harper & Row, 1974.
*Quebedeaux, Richard. *The Worldy Evangelicals.* New York: Harper & Row, 1978.
Struchen, Jeanette. *Zapped by JESUS.* New York: A. J. Holman Company, 1972.
Two Brothers from Berkeley. *Letters to Street Christians.* Grand Rapids: Zondervan Publishing House, 1971.

Music and Media
Anderson, David L. C., compiler. *The New Jesus Style Song Book.* Minneapolis: Augsburg Publishing House, 1972.
*Benson, Dennis. *Electric Evangelism.* Nashville, Tennessee: Abingdon Press, 1973.
Benson, Dennis C., *The Rock Generation.* Nashville, Tennessee: Abingdon Press, 1976.
Edmondson, Frank M., compiler. *Jubilation Songbook.* Waco, Texas: Myrrh Music, 1976.
*Larson, Bob. *Rock & Roll: The Devil's Diversion.* Carol Stream, Illinois: Creation House, 1967.
*Larson, Bob. *Rock & the Church.* Carol Stream, Illinois: Creation House, 1971.
Larson, Bob. *The Day Music Died.* Carol Stream, Illinois: Creation House, 1972.
Larson, Bob. *Hippies, Hindus and Rock and Roll.* Carol Stream, Illinois: Creation House, 1972.
*Robertson, Pat; with Jamie Buckingham. *Shout It from the Housetops.* Plainfield, New Jersey: Logos International, 1972.
Scarborough, William R., editor. *National Christian Booking and Program Directory.* New York: The Christian Booking and Program Directory, 1978. 130 W. 44th Street, New York, NY 10036.
Whitburn, Joel C., compiler. *Joel Whitburn's Top Pop Records 1955–1972* and yearly

supplements 1973–1979. Menomonee Falls, Wisconsin: Record Research, 1973 and each year thereafter. P.O. Box 82, Menomonee Falls, WI 53051.

Biographies
*Boone, Pat. *A New Song*. Carol Stream, Illinois: Creation House, 1970.
Cash, Johnny. *Man in Black*. Grand Rapids: Zondervan Publishing House, 1975.
Crouch, Andraé; with Nina Ball. *Through It All*. Waco, Texas: Word Books, 1974.
Medema, Ken; with Joyce Norman. *Come and See*. Waco, Texas: Word Books, 1976.
*Ross, Scott; with John and Elizabeth Sherrill. *Scott Free*. Old Tappan, New Jersey: Chosen Books, 1976.
*Thomas, B. J.; with Jerry B. Jenkins. *Home Where I Belong*. Waco, Texas: Word Books, 1978.
*Winter, David. *New Singer, New Song: The Cliff Richard Story*. Waco, Texas: Word Books, 1967.

Notes

Chapter 1
1. Edward E. Plowman, *The Underground Church* (Elgin, Illinois: David C. Cook Publishing Co., 1971), p. 25.
2. Billy Graham, *The Jesus Generation* (Grand Rapids, Michigan: Zondervan Publishing House, 1971), p. 24.
3. Ibid., p. 20.
4. Ibid., p. 45.
5. Dennis C. Benson, *The Now Generation* (Richmond, Virginia: John Knox Press, 1969), p. 118.
6. Ibid., p. 17.
7. Norman Vincent Peale, "The Surging Spirit," *Guideposts,* November 1971, p. 4.
8. Plowman, *Underground Church,* p. 10.
9. John 15:12 (KJV).
10. Matt. 5:9 (KJV).
11. Matt. 5:22 (KJV).
12. Peale, "Surging Spirit," p. 4.
13. "The New Rebel Cry: Jesus Is Coming," *Time,* June 21, 1971, p. 56.
14. Patrick Corman, "Freaking Out on Jesus," *Rolling Stone,* 1971, p. 24.
15. "The New Rebel Cry," p. 5.

Chapter 2
1. Darryl E. Hicks, "Thurlow Spurr—PTL's Music Man," *The Singing News,* September 1, 1978, p. 17A.
2. "He's Everything to Me" by Ralph Carmichael. © Copyright 1964 by Lexicon Music, Inc. ASCAP. All rights reserved. International copyright secured. Used by special permission.
3. "Jimmy Owens Discusses Pop Music in the Church: Part 2," *Rock In Jesus,* September/October 1972, pp. 13–14.
4. "The Salvation Army: The Band Marches On—With A Rock Beat," *Right On!,* February 1973, p. 14.

Chapter 3
1. © 1968 Paul Simon. Used by permission.
2. *Hit Parader,* January 1971, p. 27.

Chapter 4
1. W. Bender, "Rock Passion," *Time,* November 9, 1970, p. 47.
2. "Religious Rock," *New Yorker,* November 7, 1970, p. 39.

3. Ibid.
4. Bender, "Rock Passion," p. 47.
5. "Pop Testament," *Newsweek,* November 16, 1970, p. 96.
6. Ibid.
7. Cheryl A. Forbes, "Superstar; haunting questions," *Christianity Today,* December 4, 1970, pp. 38–9.
8. Ibid.
9. Clifford Edwards, "Jesus Christ Superstar: Electric Age Messiah," *Catholic World,* August 1971, p. 220.
10. "Jesus Christ Superstar review," *Business Week,* September 11, 1971, pp. 46–7.
11. "Jesus Christ Superstar review," *Time,* October 25, 1971, p. 64.
12. "Pop Testament," *Newsweek,* p. 96.
13. Cheryl A. Forbes, "From Bach to O'Horgan," *Christianity Today,* December 3, 1971, pp. 42–3.
14. "Jesus Christ Superstar review," *Time,* p. 66.
15. Billy Graham, *The Jesus Generation* (Grand Rapids, Michigan: Zondervan Publishing House, 1971), p. 131.
16. "Controversy rages over 'Superstar,' " *Planet,* March 1972, p. 26.
17. D. P. Scaer, "Jesus Christ Superstar," *Springfielder,* March 1971, p. 298.
18. Forbes, "Superstar; haunting questions," p. 39.

Chapter 6
1. Norris McWhirter, *Guiness Book of World Records* (New York: Sterling Publishing Company, Inc., 1962), Revised American Edition, 1977 p. 237.
2. Michael J. Conner, "The Electric Church," *The Wall Street Journal,* September 4, 1974, p. 32.
3. Dennis C. Benson, *The Now Generation* (Richmond, Virginia: John Knox Press, 1969), p. 17.
4. Pat Robertson with Jamie Buckingham, *Shout It From the Housetops* (Plainfield, New Jersey: Logos International, 1972), p. 202.
5. Ibid., p. 204.

Chapter 7
1. Charles M. Austin, "Honest Exuberance," *Christian Century,* August 4, 1971, p. 938.
2. Tom Prideaux, "On this rock, a little miracle," *Life,* August 4, 1972, p. 20.
3. H. Elliott Wright, "Jesus on stage: A Reappraisal," *Christian Century,* July 19, 1972, p. 786.
4. Joseph Barton, "The Godspell Story," *America,* December 11, 1971, p. 517.
5. H. Elliott Wright, "Jesus on Stage," *Christian Century,* July 19, 1972, p. 786.
6. David Brudnoy, "Hosanna!" *National Review,* August 17, 1973, p. 898.

Chapter 8
1. Cathy Steere, *Impact,* July 1972, p. 3.
2. Randy Matthews, © New Bay Psalter Music Press, Inc./Paragon Music Corp., 1975.

Chapter 11
1. Bob Larson, *Rock & The Church* (Carol Stream, Illinois: Creation House, 1971), p. 54.
2. Ibid., p. 78.
3. Ibid., p. 69.
4. Letter to the Editor, *Cornerstone,* Vol. 6, Issue 37, June/July 1977, p. 4.

Chapter 12
1. Liz Neuman. "Expectation," *Jesus '76—Mercer Program Book,* p. 5.

Chapter 13
1. Letter to the Editor, "Thankful," *Lincoln Star,* April 18, 1975.

Chapter 14
1. John Anderson, *Rolling Stone,* January 29, 1976.
2. David Winter, *New Singer, New Song* (Waco, Texas: Word Books, 1967), p. 130.
3. Jerry Hopkins, "Cliff Richard: an Elvis for Christ," *Rolling Stone,* April 13, 1972, p. 18.
4. Ibid.
5. "Just Plain Noel Stookey," *Right On!,* March 1973, p. 5.
6. Ibid.

Chapter 16
1. 1 Cor 1:18 (NASV).
2. Psalm 75:6, 7 (paraphrased).

Epilogue
1. Richard Quebedeaux, *The Worldly Evangelicals* (New York: Harper & Row, 1978), p. 168.
2. 1 Timothy 4:12.